ENGLISH WRITING FOR ACADEMIC PURPOSES
学术英语写作

余莉
陈洁　梁永刚　编著

清华大学出版社
北京

内 容 简 介

学术英语写作是高级阶段的英语学习者必须掌握的一项英语技能。本书的三位编者长期从事高校英语教学工作,切实了解学生在英语学习中的实际需求和具体困难。本着因材施教和因需施教的原则,针对学生在英语学习中的实际问题和需求,编者从国外一流学术期刊上选择了百余篇学术论文,对其进行了客观细致的语篇分析,总结出学术英语写作的基本要素和规范的语言表述方式,能为高级阶段的英语学习者及研究人员在英语学术写作方面提供卓有成效的技术指导。

版权所有,侵权必究。举报:010-62782989,beiqinquan@tup.tsinghua.edu.cn。

图书在版编目(CIP)数据

学术英语写作/余莉,陈洁,梁永刚编著. —北京:清华大学出版社,2015(2021.11重印)
ISBN 978-7-302-39448-8

Ⅰ. ①学… Ⅱ. ①余… ②陈… ③梁… Ⅲ. ①英语-写作 Ⅳ. ①H315

中国版本图书馆 CIP 数据核字(2015)第 036508 号

责任编辑:赵益鹏
封面设计:陈国熙
责任校对:刘玉霞
责任印制:沈　露

出版发行:清华大学出版社
网　　址:http://www.tup.com.cn, http://www.wqbook.com
地　　址:北京清华大学学研大厦 A 座　　　　邮　编:100084
社 总 机:010-62770175　　　　　　　　　　邮　购:010-62786544
投稿与读者服务:010-62776969, c-service@tup.tsinghua.edu.cn
质量反馈:010-62772015, zhiliang@tup.tsinghua.edu.cn

印 装 者:三河市铭诚印务有限公司
经　　销:全国新华书店
开　　本:185mm×260mm　　印　张:11.25　　字　数:269 千字
版　　次:2015 年 8 月第 1 版　　　　　　　印　次:2021 年 11 月第 10 次印刷
定　　价:32.00 元

产品编号:062289-02

前 言

随着各级英语教育改革的不断深化,因需施教的教学理念在高校英语教学实践与研究中受到越来越多的关注。如何使英语学习成为学生未来职业发展和学术深造的助推器,是每一位高校英语教师一直在思考的问题。

相对于初、中级英语教育,高校英语教育表现出两个明显的区别性特征:一是学习者的英语基础存在更大的差异,二是学习者的目的不尽相同。因此,如果在高校英语教学中仍然与在中学阶段一样采用统一的教材,制定统一的学习计划和要求,采取统一的教学方法和考核方式,则势必导致越来越多的学生对英语学习产生厌学情绪,使英语学习事倍功半。因此,我们决定编写一本能够为高级阶段英语学习者提供实际帮助的学术英语写作方面的教材。

在长期的教学实践中,通过对学生英语学习状况的观察,对学生英语学习中所存在问题的梳理与分析,对学生英语学习目的的调查与研讨,我们发现,学生在英语学习过程中,在英语写作能力方面存在更大的困惑与困难。一方面,受到母语因素和自身英语功底的影响,学生难以用恰当的英语写出符合英语行文规范的文章;另一方面,学生在日常的学习中,甚至在未来的职业生涯中似乎也并不需要写作所谓的记叙文、描写文、议论文和平常意义上的说明文,对于那些希望在学术研究方面继续深造的学生则更是如此。基于此,我们得出结论:在高校的英语学习者中确实存在对提高学术英语写作能力的需求。有鉴于此,我们从国外一流学术期刊上选择了百余篇学术论文,对其进行了客观细致的语篇分析,总结出学术英语写作的基本要素和规范的语言表述方式,同时参阅了国内目前已出版的学术英语写作教材,完成了《学术英语写作》初稿的写作并以讲义的形式在兰州交通大学部分本科生、研究生及博士生的英语教学中试用了两年。学生一致认为,这本讲义切中他们在学术英语写作中的实际问题,使用方便,对提高他们的学术英语写作水平有很大的帮助。与此同时,他们也诚恳地提出了讲义中存在的一些问题,我们已对这些问题进行了修正。

与目前国内的同类教材相比,本书略去了对学术英语写作在理论层面的探讨,直击学习者在学术英语写作中的实际问题,以最直接的方式为学习者解决具体问题提供最便捷、最直观的技术指导,既适合用作学术英语写作教材,也可作为各学科研究者撰写英语学术论文的使用指南。

本教材由兰州交通大学研究生校内教改立项课程专项资助。兰州交通大学教务处、研究生学院及外语学院的领导和老师对本书的编写和使用提出了中肯的建议和意见,外语学院研究生邹雨娟、叶艳妮、张丹华、王金凤对本书进行了严格认真的校对,清华大学出版社赵益鹏编辑对本书的出版提供了巨大的帮助,在此一并表示诚挚的感谢。因为编者水平有限,书中如有疏漏谬误之处,请各位读者谅解。

编 者
2015 年 2 月于兰州

目 录

第1章 总论	1
1.1 学术英语的基本话语特征	2
1.1.1 人称、时态和语态	2
1.1.2 长句与状语	2
1.2 学术英语的基本结构特征	3
1.3 练习题	3
第2章 摘要	6
2.1 概述	6
2.1.1 摘要的定义	6
2.1.2 摘要的作用和功能	6
2.1.3 摘要的分类与特点	6
2.2 构成要素	14
2.3 写作范式	16
2.3.1 研究主题的写作范式	16
2.3.2 研究背景的写作范式	19
2.3.3 研究目的的写作范式	21
2.3.4 研究方法的写作范式	23
2.3.5 研究结果的写作范式	25
2.3.6 研究结论的写作范式	26
2.3.7 范文分析	28
2.4 练习题	30
2.5 相关阅读	35
第3章 引言	45
3.1 概述	45
3.2 构成要素	46
3.3 写作范式	50
3.3.1 研究现状的写作范式	50
3.3.2 研究中心的写作范式	60
3.3.3 研究目的与意义的写作范式	65

　　　　3.3.4　引言全文范文分析 ··· 74
　3.4　练习题 ··· 80
　3.5　相关阅读 ··· 92

第4章　结论 ··· 100
　4.1　概述 ··· 100
　4.2　构成要素 ··· 100
　4.3　写作范式 ··· 101
　　　　4.3.1　总结与回顾的写作范式 ··· 101
　　　　4.3.2　讨论与评述的写作范式 ··· 102
　　　　4.3.3　建议与展望的写作范式 ··· 103
　　　　4.3.4　范文分析 ··· 103
　4.4　练习题 ··· 105
　4.5　相关阅读 ··· 109

第5章　致谢 ··· 115
　5.1　概述 ··· 115
　5.2　构成要素 ··· 115
　5.3　写作范式 ··· 116
　5.4　练习题 ··· 121
　5.5　相关阅读 ··· 123

附录A　文字指南 ·· 129

附录B　缩写词、数字及符号 ·· 138

附录C　国外常见文后参考文献著录格式 ··· 141

附录D　图表的使用与语言表述 ··· 142

附录E　学术英语写作常用词汇 ··· 147

参考文献 ·· 168

第1章 总论

　　学术英语目前已成为英语教育的新热点，这一现象的出现主要可归因于传统英语教育所面临的困境以及英语本身作为国际通用语的强势地位。传统的英语教育多强调英语作为一般交流工具的功能，所以其选用的教学材料多倾向于文化习俗、日常生活交往、普遍的人类情感、对人们的日常生活产生影响的社会现象以及面向普遍人群的科普材料等。这些材料基本不对任何专业领域进行深入的探究和讨论，所以被称为 General English，即普通英语。英语学习者长期浸润于这类英语学习材料中，导致的一个直接后果便是在学术研究中难以做到"学以致用"，即无法用所学的英语在相关领域内进行对话和交流，以致学习者对英语学习的意义和价值产生极大的怀疑。与此同时，英语作为国际学术界通用语言的地位又迫使非英语国家的学者必须能够熟练、规范地运用英语，去获得相关领域的最新研究成果，与国外同行进行及时、高质量的学术交流，同时将自己的研究成果在国际上加以推广。正是在这一背景下，国内高校的英语专业纷纷结合其学科特点，开设了工程实践英语、商务英语、法律英语、中医英语等学术英语类课程，获得了良好的社会效果。

　　学术英语写作是学术英语教育的一个重要组成部分，是对科学研究信息和思想的归纳和总结，是对概念、事件和现象的解释、分析、说明和评价，是对相关领域热点论题的讨论。因而，学术英语写作是衡量学生学术英语学习质量的一把重要标尺，也是学习者的学习难点。由于受到英语语言水平的限制，学习者往往很难用规范的学术英语准确介绍自己的研究成果，阐明其研究的价值和意义。同时，学术英语受其表述对象及功能的限制，又形成了独有的行文规范，在遣词、结构、句式等方面表现出很强的规律性，这无疑为学习者迅速掌握学术英语的写作要领提供了很大的可能性。由于学科门类的差异和复杂性，本教材内容涵盖了英文学术论文中的四个基本构成部分，即摘要、引言、结论和致谢。这四部分是英文学术论文的核心部分，也是学术英语写作中共性最强的部分，学习者可以通过本教材快速掌握这四个部分在写作范式上的规律性。

　　本教材对国外 50 多种重要的学术期刊论文进行了文本分析，总结、归纳出学术英语写作在构成要素和写作范式上的突出特征。同时，通过丰富的例句、范文分析及相关阅读材料，在遣词、结构、句式等方面为读者提供了直观、有效的归纳和总结，能够帮助国内研究人员快速、有效地提高学术英语写作质量。

1.1 学术英语的基本话语特征

1.1.1 人称、时态和语态

学术论文是对一项研究过程和成果的呈现和总结,多从客观的角度,用简练的语言陈述论文的主要内容。从人称代词的使用情况来看,第一人称代词的使用最为常见,而第一人称复数"we"的使用频度远远高于第一人称单数"I"的使用频度。"we"的含义有两种,第一种情况用于叙述论文作者具体完成的某种实验、观察到的现象或得出的结论等;另一种情况是为了引导读者按照作者的思路思考问题,此时"we"不再是作者自己,而是指作者和读者双方,甚至在由一位作者独立完成的学术论文中,亦常使用第一人称复数"we"。在人称代词的使用上,除了多使用"I"和"we"之外,第一人称复数宾格"us"和所有格"our"在英语学术论文中的使用频度也较高。此外,有时也会出现第二人称,通常第二人称的使用主要是为了达到启发的目的,引导读者思考某些问题,如"You might guess that it is more difficult to figure out whether a reaction is spontaneous than to determine which way a car will roll on a hill"。除第一、第二人称代词的使用情况外,无生命第三人称或者用客观对象作主语的无人称句子的使用也很普遍,因为学术论文的着眼点是客观存在的现象、性质以及实验结果和所得出的结论,而不是作者本身,因而常会用到具体名词充当主语。

在时态的使用上,最常用的四种时态是一般现在时、一般过去时、现在完成时和一般将来时。作者需要根据表达的意图选择恰当的时态,如一般现在时可以用于表达对相关领域的关注、研究目的等;一般过去时和现在完成时可以用于回顾前人研究成果、指出前人研究的不足;陈述研究方法和步骤则多使用一般过去时;描述研究的前景和方向则使用一般将来时等。

采用何种语态,既要考虑具体学术论文的特点,又要满足语言表达的需要。相较其他文体,被动语态的使用是英文学术论文的一个突出特征,因为被动语态可以把所讨论的对象放在主语位置,这样更加引人注目。撰写者需要注意的是,应按需选择使用主动语态或被动语态。主动语态多用于描述动作,而被动语态则多用于表达状态、结果和性质。此外,被动语态陈述的口吻更为客观,文体上更为正式,这也在一定程度上符合英文学术论文这一特殊学术文体的需要。

1.1.2 长句与状语

英语动词有十六个时态,对于非英语专业的学习者来说,想运用自如这些时态是有困难的。为了弥补这些不足,可以尝试使用更多状语从句。长句是学术英语中一个突出的话语特征。长句结构严密,表达信息丰富,层次多样,但长句并不意味着复杂的语法句型,可以通过加入状语或状语从句来实现,当然还可以添加定语、定语从句以及名词性结构等来表达更丰富的内容。需要注意的是,在学术论文阅读和写作的过程中,首先要确定主句,然后找到主句中的主语和谓语,最后将着眼点放在从句和其他成分,这样在一定程度上能够帮助我们有效地解读和流畅地撰写英文学术论文。

英文学术论文要突出科学性、严谨性、客观性,避免使用文学性、艺术性和主观性的文字,但是并不意味着英文学术论文不讲求文采。这里的文采指的是语言流畅、段落分明、叙述简洁、逻辑严密等。

1.2 学术英语的基本结构特征

学术论文通常遵循 IMRD 框架模式,即"引言部分(Introduction)、方法部分(Methodology)、结果部分(Results)、讨论部分(Discussion)"。为了达到学术论文的交际目的,每一部分又由不同的写作要素构成,而这些内在的构成要素因研究内容、方法、目的、性质、背景、对象、学科等诸多因素的不同而呈现出一定差异。内在的构成要素通常可以分为必须性部分(obligatory)和选择性部分(optional)。因此,充分了解每一部分的核心构成要素对于正确、有效地阅读和撰写英文学术论文至关重要。

1. 摘要的结构特征

一篇较为完备的摘要应该向读者准确、凝练、清晰地提供和介绍论文的主要内容,以便读者对论文的意义和价值做出大致的判断。摘要通常包含以下结构要素:(1)论文主题;(2)研究背景;(3)研究目的;(4)研究方法;(5)研究结果;(6)研究结论。

2. 引言的结构特征

作为英文学术论文正文的第一部分,引言部分的写作对于本族语者和非本族语者而言都是困难丛生。充分了解引言的结构特征及构成要素对于有效、流畅地写作引言至关重要。可将引言的宏观结构归纳为以下三个部分:(1)研究现状;(2)研究中心;(3)研究的目的和意义。对于每一个部分的内在构成,又分别由不同的具体要素来实现。在写作过程中,可以根据自身研究的特点、性质对具体要素进行选择和组合。引言可以由一段或多段文字构成,其篇幅主要取决于研究的性质、特点和约稿的要求等因素。

3. 结论的结构特征

结论位于论文正文最后,应概括、总结论文中所提及的内容。结论通常包含以下构成要素:(1)总结和回顾;(2)讨论和评述;(3)建议和展望。

1.3 练习题

1. 简要描述英文学术论文的话语特征。
2. 英文学术论文的结构特征是什么?
3. 英文学术论文的摘要、引言、结论部分的结构特征分别是什么?
4. 简要分析以下两篇引言的人称、时态、语态。

I

The moves of a group of European countries toward more integrated financial markets and a single European currency, the Euro, raise the issue of what is an optimal currency area. This further raises the question of whether the Euro Area countries form a common currency area. This is a very timely question because the Euro is currently scheduled to replace national currencies in the Euro Area in 2002.

Most of the previous discussion about optimal currency areas has been couched in macroeconomic or political terms. Since Mudell originated the concept of an optimum currency area, the debate in economics has focused on the macroeconomic aspects of a common currency area. Malchup points out "there have been a good many attempts to define the concept of an 'optimum currency area'. The originally proposed definition was in terms of internal mobility and external mobility of productive factors—perfect intraregional immigration of labor and unrestrained outflow and inflow of capital funds. Other definitions have been in terms of mutual compatibilities of the member countries in matters of economic institutions and coordination of national policies, in the complementarity of their trade patterns, and similar criteria." Malchup himself takes a political view, saying "Pragmatically, therefore, an optimum currency area is a region no part of which insists on creating money and having a monetary policy of its own." More recently, Cohen couched his discussion of the costs and benefits of a European common currency in terms of macroeconomic policy.

By concentrating on macroeconomic and political criteria, previous researchers have ignored the requirements that economic theory places on optimizing behavior for any area to have a common currency. In this paper, these microeconomic foundations for the existence of an optimum currency area are set forth. These microeconomic criteria for the existence of an optimum currency area are similar to the criteria for the existence of an aggregate that might be called money in a single country. In the following section these criteria are set forth.

II

Insights into the behavior of pedestrians, and tools to predict this behavior, are essential in the planning and design of public pedestrian facilities such as airports, transfer stations, and shopping malls. Also, when designing timetables for public transit, pedestrian simulation models can be applied to analyze the impact of pedestrian flows between access and egress points (train platforms, bus station, etc.), entries and exits, on the walking times, and pedestrian comfort levels. Managing pedestrian flows through these facilities, for instance by information provision, requires knowledge of the pedestrian flow characteristics as well as of the walking behavior that constitutes the flow. To perform (ex ante) model studies, simulation models predicting pedestrian flows in the walking facilities can be used. A number of simulation tools have been developed for this purpose, for example, PEDROUTE and PAXPORT, SimPed, NOMAD, and Leginon. These models have been applied with success to assist in the evaluation or optimization of designs of new or existing walking facilities. Whether such pedestrian simulation models are used, or whether walking infrastructure design is carried out by other means, it is obvious that good insights into macroscopic feature of the pedestrian flows, as well as insights into the microscopic behavior underlying these features, are very important.

This article describes new and important experimental findings of pedestrian flow theory, in particular, pertaining to behavior of pedestrians and characteristics of pedestrian flows in the case of bottle necks. To this end, a brief state-of-the-art overview is presented first. In section 3, the experimental design is discussed. Section 4 provides insight into the relations between pedestrian behavior and the macroscopic characteristics of the pedestrian flow. Section 5 provides an overview of the various phenomena that have been observed from the bottleneck experiments (spatial distribution of pedestrians, swaying, dynamic layer formation, and patterns inside the bottleneck). In section 6, composite headway models—differentiating between free and constrained headways—are successfully estimated. Section 7 discusses the implication of the findings to bottleneck capacity analysis.

5. 按照摘要的篇章结构特征简要分析下面的摘要。

Abstract

This paper was presented in part by V. L. Snoeyink as the Simon w. Freese Lecture at the 2002 Canadian Society of Civil Engineer/Environmental and Water Resources Institute of ASCE Environmental Engineering Conference in Niagara Falls, Ontario, Canada, July 22, 2002. The interactions of corroded iron pipe surfaces with water are of importance because they can lead to serious water quality degradation and material deterioration. A conceptual model has been developed in this paper to describe the formation and growth of iron scales, and their reactions that lead to colored water problems. Most corrosion scales have characteristic structural features, such as a loosely held top surface layer, a shell-like layer(s) and a porous core. According to this model corrosion scales are expected to grow from inside the scale via the corrosion reaction, i.e., the conversion of iron metal to ferrous iron. The average oxidation state of iron increases with distance from the pipe wall. The scale structure and scale reactions permit the ferrous iron to be released to the bulk water, where it undergoes conversion to particular ferric iron, which is the cause of colored water. Scale structure and composition play important roles in the reactions of iron scales that lead to iron release, and water quality control to decrease the porosity of the scale is an important means of reducing iron release. It is anticipated that the conceptual model presented here will be used as a basis for changing water quality to minimize colored water formation, and as a guide for further research.

第2章 摘要

2.1 概述

2.1.1 摘要的定义

摘要又称为概要、内容提要,是以提供论文内容梗概为目的,不加评论和补充解释,简明扼要地叙述论文重要内容的短文,是对论文内容的高度概述和浓缩。摘要通常介于论文题目与正文之间,是科技论文必不可少的一个重要组成部分。

摘要虽然置于正文之前,但通常是写完整篇论文之后再撰写摘要,这样论文作者就能够用清晰凝练的语言表述论文中最重要的部分;摘要中不宜使用图表,不宜举例。

2.1.2 摘要的作用和功能

摘要应具有独立性和自明性,并且拥有与论文等量的主要信息,即不阅读全文,就能获得必要的信息。摘要已经成为学术论文写作中必不可少的组成部分,其主要功能如下:

(1) 让读者尽快了解论文的主要内容,以补充论文题目所提供信息的不足。现代科技文献信息浩如烟海,读者检索到论文题目后是否决定阅读全文,主要是通过阅读摘要来判断。所以,摘要担负着吸引读者和介绍文章主要内容的任务。

(2) 为科技情报文献检索数据库的建设和维护提供方便。论文发表后,文摘、杂志或各种数据库对摘要可以不作修改或稍作修改而直接利用。随着计算机技术和互联网的迅猛发展,网上查询、检索和下载专业数据已成为当前科技信息情报检索的重要手段,网上各类全文数据库、文摘数据库越来越显示出现代社会信息交流的水平和发展趋势。同时,论文摘要的索引是读者检索文献的重要工具,所以论文摘要的质量直接影响着论文的被检索率和被引用频次。

2.1.3 摘要的分类与特点

论文摘要的撰写有其自身的规律,但是每一篇摘要也有不同于其他摘要的特点。在撰写论文摘要时,应充分考虑到不同摘要各自的特点。

摘要可按以下方法进行分类。

1. 按照论文撰写和发表的目的和用途进行分类
1) 学术刊物论文摘要

正式学术刊物通常均要求论文作者提供中英文摘要,关于这类摘要的篇幅,各学术期刊的要求虽略有差别,但大多限定为 150～200 字。内容通常包括研究目的、研究方法、研究结果和主要结论。

参见下例:

Abstract

The aim of this article is to determine with real data to what extent the hypotheses on which Clement's first formula is based are fulfilled, and to compare the results of applying this formula. To this end the flow demand in the peak period was studied in two distribution networks with different irrigation methods and crops located in the Ebro River basin (northeast Spain). The calibration procedure for this formula proposed by the Center Technique du Genie Rural des Eaux et des Forest (CTGREF) in 1977 was also analyzed. The result was that most of the hypotheses were not fulfilled. Furthermore, the discharge distributions obtained in the period of study did not correspond to a normal distribution. However, comparing the real accumulated probability curve and that calculated by Clement's formula, it was found that the differences between the two curves for probabilities greater than 90% (a wide range of application of the formula) were lower than 9.4%. The reason for this result was found. It was shown also, that the CTGREF adjustment procedure did not provide substantial improvement in the estimation of flows because the aim of the fit was to achieve a normal distribution rather than an accumulated distribution function.

(*Journal of Irrigation and Drainage Engineering*)

2) 学术会议论文摘要

会议论文摘要往往在会议召开之前几个月撰写,目的是交给会议论文评审委员会评阅,从而决定该论文是否能够录用。所以,这类摘要应比上述第一种摘要略为详细,其字数为 200～300 字。会议论文摘要的开头有必要简单介绍一下研究课题的意义、目的和宗旨等。如果在撰写摘要时,研究工作尚未完成,全部研究结果还未得到,那么,应在方法、目的、宗旨和假设等方面多花笔墨。

参见下例:

Abstract

Introduction: African-American women (AA) have a lower incidence of breast cancer, yet a higher breast cancer mortality rate than Caucasian women (C). Whether the mortality differences are the result of more aggressive tumors in AA women or the effect of differences in socioeconomic status (SES) is debatable. A clearer understanding of the role of race requires SES to be controlled as a potential confounder, which can be achieved by evaluating outcome within a population with a high proportion of uninsured patients. Our state-run academic medical center serves as a healthcare safety net for the 715 000 uninsured residents of Louisiana. We provide compelling evidence that race is not predictive of outcome for patients with operable breast cancer.

Methods: From our prospective breast cancer database which has been maintained since 1998, we examined the data for all 803 patients with stage 0 to 3 breast cancer. All patients received standard definitive surgical care as well as appropriate adjuvant treatment. Study homogeneity was maintained by standardized treatment, surveillance, and compliance protocols. Primary endpoints were cancer recurrence and death. Statistical analysis performed included Kaplan-Meier survival analysis, log-rank test, Cox proportional hazard model, independent samples t-test, and chi-square test. A p-value 0.05 was considered statistically significant.

Results: Sixty percent of patients were AA ($N=479$ patients) and the mean follow-up time for AA and C patients was 58 months. Almost 70% of patients were classified as either free care or Medicaid. There were no significant differences in tumor size ($p=0.83$), nodal distribution ($p=0.74$), stage distribution ($p=0.88$), or definitive surgery performed ($p=0.32$) between the races. However, AA tend to be younger ($p=0.003$) with a higher tumor grade ($p<0.0001$) than C. The 5-yr overall survival (OS) and disease-free survival (DFS) for the entire cohort was 81% and 68%, respectively. For node-negative disease, the 5-yr OS and DFS was 90% and 78%, respectively ($p<0.0001$), and for node-positive disease, it was 70% and 54%, respectively ($p<0.0001$). The 5-yr OS for stages 0, 1, 2, 3 was 100%, 93%, 83%, and 61%, respectively ($p<0.0001$), and the DFS for stages 0, 1, 2, 3 was 85%, 82%, 71%, and 43%, respectively ($p<0.0001$). These results were comparable with the National Cancer Database. The impact of race on outcome was as follows: The 5-yr OS for AA and C was 80% and 83% ($p=0.21$), respectively, and the 5-yr DFS for AA and C was 69% and 65% ($p=0.19$), respectively. For stage 0, the 5-yr OS was 100% for both AA and C and the 5-yr DFS was 85% for AA and 84% for C ($p=0.90$). For stage 1, the 5-yr OS was 91% for AA and 93% for C ($p=0.41$), and the 5-yr DFS was 82% for AA and 80% for C ($p=0.32$). For stage 2, the 5-yr OS was 81% for AA and 86% for C ($p=0.18$), and the 5-yr DFS was 72% for AA and 68% for C ($p=0.29$). For stage 3, the 5-yr OS was 59% for AA and 61% for C ($p=0.67$), and the 5-yr DFS was 45% for AA and 38% for C ($p=0.35$). On multivariate analysis, race was not an independent predictor of cancer recurrence ($p=0.11$) or cancer death ($p=0.22$).

Conclusion: In a predominantly indigent population, race had no impact on breast cancer outcome. Hence, women who were treated at our academic center with a public hospital can expect to have breast cancer outcome rivaling those reported in the literature. Further study is needed to understand the elements involved in our success.

(*Second AACR International Conference on the Science of Cancer Health Disparities*— *Feb* 3-6, 2009; *Carefree, AZ*)

3）学位论文摘要

学位论文是表明论文作者从事科学研究取得创造性的结果或有了新的见解，并以此为内容撰写成文，作为申请授予相应的学位时考核评审用的学术论文。学位论文分为学士论文、硕士论文和博士论文三个级别，三种论文对学术水平以及对论文的深度和广度虽有不同要求，但学士、硕士和博士论文摘要一般都要求用中、英文两种语言撰写。学位论文摘要的字数可因不同级别的论文体现差异，内容也可根据需要分为几个段落。学位论文摘要的内容一般包括研究背景、意义，主旨和目的，基本理论依据、基本假设，研究方法，研究结果，主要创新点和简短讨论等。学位论文摘要应突出新观点、新见解和新方法。

参见下例：

（1）学士学位论文摘要

Abstract

During the last decades, scientific research has revealed that the size and morphology of materials have great influence on the materials' property and characterization. Compared with bulk materials, nanomaterials have many novel properties such as quantum size effect, surface effect, etc., due to the decrease of the size of materials and the increase of the unsaturated dangling bonds and lattice defects. All of these indicate that nanomaterials have potential applications in various fields such as electromagnetics, optics and catalysis, etc. Gas sensor is one of important components in the field of automatic control. Higher demands of modification are rising for the performances of the as-prepared gas sensors, including the detection limit and the specific response of sample gas. New generation of gas sensors which are based on the semiconductor metal oxides such as SnO_2 and ZnO have shown upstanding foreground in the application field, due to their unique structures with excellent physical and chemical properties. This thesis has reported the synthesis hierarchical nanostructure of ZnO nanoparticles. Also this thesis has reported the synthesis of various kinds of ZnO nanostructures via different solvothermal processes. Structure characterization was taken on ZnO nanostructures via XRD, TEM and HRTEM, etc. Based on those existing literatures, LSS phase-transfer method is introduced to synthesize cubic phase SnO_2 nanoparticles and nanorods. Various kinds of SnO_2 nanorods doped with different kinds of ions have been synthesized via the analogous method. Also, this thesis has reported the synthesis of branched-SnO_2 nanorods which were induced by as-synthesized noble metal nanoparticles via a two steps method. Finally, the gas sensor properties of as-mentioned materials have been studied carefully and we find that minor doping of Pd will improve the character of SnO_2 gas sensor properties prominently.

(http://oaps.lib.tsinghua.edu.cn/handle/123456789/1366)

(2) 硕士学位论文摘要

Abstract

Third generation wireless mobile communication networks are characterized by the increasing utilization of data services—E-mail, web browsing, video streaming, etc. Such services allow the transition of the network from circuit switched to packet switched operation (circuit switched operation will still be supported), resulting in increased overall network performance.

These new data services require increased bandwidth and data throughput, due to their intrinsic nature. Examples are graphics-intensive web browsing and video streaming, the latter being delay sensitive and requiring priority over less sensitive services such as E-mail. This increasing demand for bandwidth and throughput has driven the work of third generation standardization committees, resulting in the specification of improved modulation and coding schemes, besides the introduction of more advanced link quality control mechanisms.

Among the several proposals for the evolution from 2G to 3G, GPRS (General Packet Radio Services) and EDGE (Enhanced Data Rates for GSM Evolution) stand out as transitional solutions for existing TDMA IS-136 and GSM networks (they are also referred to as 2.5G systems). In the CDMA arena, WCDMA (Wideband CDMA) has emerged as the most widely adopted solution, with CDMA 2000, an evolution from IS-95, also being considered.

This thesis compiles and analyzes the results of the work by the standardization committees involved in the specification of 3G standards, focusing on the receiver performance in the presence of additive noise, fading and interference. Such performance results will ultimately determine design and optimization conditions for 3G networks.

This document concerns the description of the TDMA-based 2.5G solutions that allow the introduction of multimedia and enhanced data services to existing 2G networks. It focuses on GPRS and EDGE. It also addresses WCDMA—a 3G spread spectrum solution. Such proposals permit the utilization of existing spectrum with increased efficiency, yielding extended network capacity and laying the ground for full support of wireless multimedia applications. The study is focused on the link implementation aspect of these solutions, showing the impact of the modulation schemes and link quality control mechanisms on the performance of the radio link.

(http://scholar.lib.vt.edu/theses/available/etd-05062002-143129/)

(3) 博士学位论文摘要

Abstract

This research aims at enhancing the accuracy of land vehicular navigation systems by integrating GPS and Micro-Electro-Mechanical-System (MEMS) based inertial measurement units (IMU). This comprises improving the MEMS-based inertial output signals as well as investigating the limitations of a conventional Kalman Filtering (KF) solution for MEMS-IMU/GPS integration. These limitations are due to two main reasons. The first is that a KF suppresses the effect of inertial sensor noise using GPS-derived position and velocity as updates but within a limited band of frequency. The second reason is that a KF only works well under certain predefined dynamic models and convenient input data that fit these models, which are not attainable with the utilization of MEMS-based inertial technology. Therefore, if the GPS reference solutions are lost, the accuracy of standalone MEMS-IMU navigation will drastically degrade over time.

The Wavelet Multi-Resolution Analysis (WMRA) technique is proposed in this thesis as an efficient pre-filter for MEMS-based inertial sensors outputs. Applying this pre-filtering process successfully improves the sensors' signal-to-noise ratios, removes short-term errors mixed with motion dynamics, and provides more reliable data to the KF-based MEMS-INS/GPS integration module. The results of experimental validation show the effectiveness of the proposed WMRA method in improving the accuracy of KF estimated navigation states particularly position. Moreover, the Adaptive-Neuro-Fuzzy-inference-system (ANFIS)-based algorithm is suggested and assessed to model the variations of the MEMS sensors' performance characteristics with temperature. The focus is on modeling the gyro thermal variations since it usually dominates the attainable accuracy of INS standalone navigation. Initial results show the efficiency and precision of the proposed ANFIS modeling algorithm. Finally, a new technique augmenting the powerful ANFIS predictor with the traditional KF for improving the integrated MEMS-INS/GPS system performance is presented. The proposed augmentation is utilized either to provide direct corrections to the estimated position by KF during standalone inertial navigation or to supply estimated reference position and velocity error measurements during the absence of GPS solutions, thus keeping the functionality of the KF update engine. Initial test results show the significance of the proposed ANFIS-KF augmentation in reducing position and velocity drifts during GPS outages.

(http://www.geomatics.ucalgary.ca/links/GradTheses.html)

4) 脱离原文而独立发表的摘要

这种摘要更应该具有独立性、自含性和完整性。读者无须阅读全文,便可以了解全文的主要内容。

参见下例:

Abstract

The translation of fictional names should observe a different and more flexible theory from the translation of real names, since writers often infuse meaning other than a mere signifier of a character in the appellation of their characters. In her seven novels published so far, Toni Morrison, for example, has employed a variety of appellation for her characters. Theses unorthodox and symbolically loaded names, and in some cases, the absence of names, contributed to her characterization, plotting and theme revelation. Much, if not all, of the flavor of the names will be lost with the transliteration of them into Chinese. It is, therefore, sometimes more adequate to translate their meaning into equivalent Chinese characters or phrases, to find a Chinese character or phrase that can keep the original implication in one way or another, or simply leave the English name as it is, giving an explanation in an annotation or an afterword. Chinese translation of fictional names deliberately taken from the *Bible* should be kept identical to the authoritative Chinese version of the *Bible*, and because of cultural differences, it is necessary to give a brief explanation to the biblical character by the same name.

(*Abstracts of Chinese Translation Studies*(2001))

2. 按照摘要的不同功能进行分类

1) 信息型摘要

信息型摘要，即报道型摘要，也称为资料型摘要，是指明一篇论文的主题范围及内容梗概的简明摘要，相当于简介。这类摘要一般用来反映学术论文的目的、主题、方法、主要结果和结论等，在有限的字数内向读者提供尽可能多的定性或定量的信息，充分反映该研究的创新之处。信息型摘要常见于学术性期刊或论文集，篇幅长度一般以6～7句为宜，字数通常限定在200字左右。

参见下例：

Abstract

The hydrodynamics of a rubble-mound weir are theoretically and experimentally examined. This type of weir is considered to be environmentally friendly, since its permeability allows substances and aquatic life to pass through longitudinally. By performing a one-dimensional analysis on a steady nonuniform flow through the weir, discharge is described as a function of related parameters, such as flow depth on the top-and-downstream sides of the weir, porosity, and grain diameter of the rubble mound, weir length, etc. A laboratory experiment is carried out to determine the empirical coefficients included in the analytic model. The theoretical solution of the discharge is compared with the experimental data to verify the analysis. It is confirmed that agreement between theory and experiment is satisfactory for a wide range of flow conditions. The present study makes it possible to apply the rubble mound weir for practical use as a discharge control system.

(*Journal of Hydraulic Engineering*)

该摘要第1句指明了研究的主题；第2句概括了该研究的重要性及必要性；第3～5句说明了该研究所采用的方法；第6句为研究结果，证实该研究的主要发现；第7句是研究结论，阐明该研究成果所蕴含的意义和用途。

2）指示型摘要

指示型摘要，也称为介绍型摘要、说明型摘要、描述型摘要、陈述型摘要或论点型摘要，主要介绍研究所取得成果的性质以及成果水平，使读者对该研究的主要内容有一个轮廓性的了解，不涉及论据和结论。指示型摘要一般不介绍论文的研究方法、研究结果等具体内容，不交代任何研究数据。此类摘要多适用于学术期刊的简报等。该类型的摘要一般仅包含 2~3 个简单句，概括论文的主题，言简意赅，篇幅紧凑，字数通常为 30~50 字。

参见下例：

Abstract

We present uniqueness and reciprocity theorems for linear thermo-electro-magneto-elasticity without making restrictions on the positive definiteness of the elastic moduli. The application of the reciprocity theorem is also discussed.

(*The Quarterly Journal of Mechanics & Applied Mathematics*)

该摘要仅包含短短 2 个句子，29 个单词，只是简要点明该研究的主题及用途，不作具体的介绍，未作定性或定量的分析说明，言简意赅。其缺点也是显而易见的——所提供的信息量太少。

3）信息-指示型摘要

信息-指示型摘要是一种混合型摘要，即同时兼具信息型摘要和指示型摘要的特征，以信息型摘要的形式表述学术论文中价值最高的那部分内容，其余部分则以指示型摘要的形式进行了表述。这类摘要的篇幅略长于指示型摘要，以 100~150 字为宜。

参见下例：

Abstract

The influent and effluent water quality of two ponds at four aquaculture facilities (two intensive and two semiintensive growout systems) located on the Northwest coast of Mexico was monitored. Temperature, salinity, pH, dissolved oxygen, biochemical oxygen demand (self-consumption in 48 hours), total suspended solids, particulate organic material, nitrite, nitrate, ammonium, reactive and total phosphate, and chlorophyll *a* were analyzed every 2 weeks during two consecutive growout cycles. Change recorded in most of these water quality variables were not strongly related to management practices of the ponds, but rather to environmental factors. The mean percent differences between inflowing and outflowing water that were observed indicated that water used for culture returned to the natural environment depleted of nutrients (inorganic nitrogen and reactive phosphate), and it was evident that the rearing activities promoted the exportation of particulate material to the surrounding environment.

(*Water Environment Research*)

该摘要第 1、2 句对研究主题做了较为细致的介绍；第 3、4 句介绍了研究结果和得出的结论。

以上 3 种类型是撰写摘要时普遍适用的基本模式，可供论文作者选择使用。论文作者也可以根据学术期刊的具体要求选择使用其中的某种类型。向学术性期刊投稿一般多选用信息型摘要。

2.2 构成要素

一篇完备的摘要应该向读者准确、凝练、清晰地提供、介绍论文的主要内容。摘要通常由以下要素构成。

1. 研究主题

即该研究要解决的问题，是对论文的研究核心进行的精练概述。

例1　**This paper presents an innovative model for** scheduling, resource planning, and cost optimization of large construction and/or maintenance programs that involve multiple distributed sites.

本文提出一种用以……的创新模式。

例2　**This article discusses experimental findings of** microscopic pedestrian behavior in case of bottlenecks.

本文讨论了……的实验结果。

2. 研究背景

研究背景即在该领域内，前人所从事的研究以及当前所存在的问题。

例1　**The paper provides a brief history of** scenario planning as it emerged from business-strategic planning activities and gives an overview of its goals and limitations. **The paper then reviews the context for** scenario-planning in regional transportation planning as well as precedents of its application in this field.

本文先简要回顾了……的历史，接着，本文回顾了……的背景。

例2　**Several writers have reported that** this irrigation system **has the potential to** conserve water as compared to level-basin irrigation. **However, no comparative studies on** the performance of both irrigation systems **are available, and** the stimulation of level furrows **has not been attempted. In this work**, two field experiments are reported…

据先前多位研究人员所述，……仍有潜在可能……；然而，在……方面尚无同类研究可供(参考)；对……也未予以尝试。在本研究中，……

3. 研究目的

研究目的即陈述为什么要从事该研究，着重说明研究工作的缘起。

例1　**The primary objectives of the investigation are to** assess the bridge's loading-carry capacity and compare this capacity with current standard of safety.

本论文的主要研究目的是……

例2　**The purpose of this paper is to** examine critically the implications of the new categories and paradigm shift in light of the main purpose protected areas, to protect wild biodiversity.

本文旨在……

4. 研究方法

研究方法即对研究过程中所采用的技术、手段、方法以及工具、器械、仪表等进行简要的说明，有时也应对所采用的原理和定律予以简明扼要的描述。

例1 The proposed scheduling model（DSM）**employs an information system to store data** related to various work sites, activities' optional construction methods, and available resources. The DSM **also incorporates** a scheduling **algorithm** that is resource focused, and maintains crew work continuity under any sequence of distributed sites. **To minimize cost and meet project time and resource constraints**, the DSM **uses** genetic **algorithm to** determine the optimum set of construction methods and optimum routing order among sites.

……采用了信息系统来存储数据……。……还结合了……算法。为降低造价，不误工期，节约资源……采用……算法来……

例2 **In order to examine the importance of** pre-selection criteria, **a questionnaire survey has been conducted with clients** who are responsible for pre-selecting their consultants and consultants being pre-selected by the clients.

为检验……的重要性，向客户实施了问卷调查……

5. 研究结果

研究结果即对研究所获得的实验数据、实验现象、实验结果或推理得到的理论结果进行简要描述。

例1 **Key findings of the study include**：（1）the relative importance of the top four skills（spreadsheets, word processors, computer-aid design, electric communication）has remained unchanged;（2）programming competence is ranked very low by practitioners;（3）the importance and use of geographic information system and specialized engineering software have increased over the past decade;（4）the importance and use of expert system have significantly decreased over the past decade;（5）the importance and use of equation solvers and databases have declined over the past decade.

该研究的主要发现包括……。

例2 Measured flexural strains **showed** a strain discontinuity at the glulam-concrete interface **as expected**.

与预期一致，……显示……

6. 研究结论

研究结论即对研究成果所蕴含的意义、用途，以及该研究与其他同类研究之间的关系进行概述。

例1 **Overall, the results suggest improvements to** system operation and water allocations with a statewide expected value potentially as high as $1.3 billion/year. **Significant improvements in performance appear possible through** water transfer and exchanges, conjunctive use, and various operational changes to increase flexibility. **These changes also greatly reduce costs to** agricultural and urban users of accommodating environmental requirements. **Model results also suggest benefits for** expanding selected conveyance and storage facilities.

总之，研究结果表明了在……方面的诸多改进。通过……，有望在性能方面取得巨大的改进。该变化同样大大降低了……的造价。模型结果表明对……同样有益。

例2 **The outcome of the investigation is to provide** structural **information that will**

assist the preservation of the historic John A. Roebling suspension bridge, though the developed methodology could be applied to a wide range of cable-supported bridges.

该调查的结果定将为……提供……信息，该信息将有助于……

2.3 写作范式

每篇摘要都有别于其他摘要，因此，在撰写论文摘要时，应充分考虑到每篇摘要的具体特点。但是，论文摘要的写作也有其共性规律，其所包含要素的写作通常都有一定的范式可以遵循。

2.3.1 研究主题的写作范式

研究主题即该研究要解决的问题，是对论文的研究核心进行精练的概述。介绍论文研究主题时常用到的表达范式如表 2-1 所示。

表 2-1 研究主题的写作范式

This article/analysis/ essay/investigation/ paper/research/study/ survey/thesis/ work, etc.	addresses…	本文探讨了……
	analyzes…	本文分析了……
	argues/deems/holds…	本文认为……
	concerns…	本文关注了……
	covers/includes…	本文涵盖了……
	deals with/touches on …	本文涉及……
	is about…	本文是关于……的研究
The author	demonstrates…	作者演示了……
	discusses…	作者讨论了……
	describes…	作者描述了……
	elaborates on/expounds …	作者详述了……
	emphasizes…	作者强调了……
	explains…	作者阐明了……
	explores/probes into …	作者探究了……
	expresses…	作者阐述了……
	focuses on…	作者关注了……
	formulates…	作者阐述了……
	introduces/presents …	作者介绍了……
	investigates…	作者调查研究了……
	monitors…	作者监测了……
	presents…	作者陈述了……
	provides…	作者提出了……
	reports…	作者报道了……
	reveals…	作者揭示了……
	suggests…	作者认为……
	shows/exhibits …	作者展示了……
	studies…	作者研究了……
	summarizes…	作者总结陈述了……
…	is studied in this paper	本文研究了……
	is the subject of this investigation	该研究的主题是……

参见下例：

例1　**To this end** the flow demand in the peak period **was studied** in two distribution networks with different irrigation methods and crops located in the Ebro River basin (northeast Spain). The calibration procedure for this formula **proposed by** the Center Technique du Genie Rural des Eaux et des Forest (CTGREF) in 1977 **was also analyzed**.

出于……目的，研究了……。同时，还分析了由……提出的……

例2　A dowel-type shear connector for achieving composite action in glulam bridge girders supporting a concrete deck **is described**.

（本文）描述了……

例3　**This paper develops** probabilistic and human reliability **models to estimate the probability of** structural collapse during the construction of typical multistory reinforced-concrete buildings in the presence of human error.

本文研发了……的模式用以估量……的概率。

例4　**A** 3D finite-element **model is developed to** represent the bridge and to establish its deformed equilibrium configuration due to dead loading.

本文研发了……的模式用以……

例5　**This article discusses experimental findings of** microscopic pedestrian behavior in case of bottlenecks.

本文讨论了……的实验结果。

例6　**By using** the global positioning system (GPS), **a novel** train detection **system has been established to** assist trains with carbody tilt control.

本文借助……确立了一种全新的……系统用以……

例7　**This analysis examines the historical relationship between** land-use **and** the location of capacity-increasing highway projects in Oregon from 1970 to 1990.

本解析验证了……与……之间的历史关系。

例8　**The** hydrodynamics **of** a rubble-mound weir **are theoretically and experimentally examined**.

本文从理论与实验两方面检验了……

例9　**We introduce a novel design methodology which consists of** pre-and post-processing techniques that enable EC with minimal perturbation.

本文引入了一种新的设计方法，该方法包括……

例10　**The paper looks at the problem of** intercepting an out-of-communication team member **and describes ways of using** planning **to** reduce communication distance in anticipation of a break in connection.

本文审视了……问题，同时描述了用……来……的诸多途径。

例11　**A** combined **model of** interregional, multimodal commodity shipments, incorporating regional input-output relationship, and the associated transportation network flows **is formulated as an alternative to** the four-step travel forecasting procedure of trip generation, distribution, mode choice, and assignment.

本文阐述了一种用作……替代方案的模式。

例 12 **The paper investigates the application of** robust, nonlinear observation and control strategies, namely sliding mode observation and control (SMOC), to semiactive vehicle suspensions **using a** model reference **approach.**

本文借助……方法,调查了……的应用情况。

例 13 **This paper presents an innovative model for** scheduling, resource planning, and cost optimization of large construction and/or maintenance programs that involve multiple distributed sites.

本文提出一种用以……的创新模式。

例 14 **A** micromechanical **model** for the steady-state deformation of idealized asphalt mixes **is presented.**

本文提出一种用以……的模式。

例 15 **This paper proposes a framework for using** business and organizational scenario-planning techniques **for** regional strategic transportation-planning purposes.

本文提出一种借用……来……的框架体系。

例 16 **A model for** optimizing the allocation of resources based on the operational reliability of transport network system **is proposed.**

本文提出一种用以……的模式。

例 17 **In this paper, we prove that** range block mean and contrast scaling parameters are independent.

在本文中,笔者证实……

例 18 **We provide an analysis of** available redundancy remaining in two compressed video data.

本文分析了……

例 19 **This paper shows how** moving obstructions in (kinematic wave) traffic streams can be modeled with "off the shelf" computer program.

本文展示了……如何……

例 20 The behavior of a nano-scale cylindrical body (e.g., a fiber), lying on a substrate and acted upon by a combination of normal and tangential forces, **is the subject of this investigation.**

本研究的主题是……

例 21 Sensitivity analysis method for transport systems having an automobile road network and a physically separate transmit network **are studied.**

本文研究了……

例 22 **This investigation treats** the two-dimensional plane strain elastic deformation of both the cylinder and the substrate during a rolling/sliding motion, **including** the effect adhesion using the Maugis model.

本研究探讨了……,包括……

2.3.2 研究背景的写作范式

研究背景即前人在该领域所做的研究及当前尚存的空白。介绍论文研究背景时常用到的表达范式如下。

1. 背景回顾（见表 2-2）

表 2-2 背景回顾的写作范式

... have developed dramatically over the last century, lessons learned...	在过去的一个世纪里，……发生了翻天覆地的变化，从中可以汲取的经验教训是……
In the previous publication it was shown ...	先前发表的（论文）中表述了……
This paper presents the results of... surveys conducted by...	该论文呈现了由……所开展的……调查结果
The paper provides a brief history of...	文章简要回顾了……的历史
The paper reviews the context for...	文章回顾了……的背景

参见下例：

例 1 **This paper presents the results of** two **surveys conducted by** the American Society of Civil Engineers' Task Committee on Computing Education of the Technique Council on Computing and Information Technology to assess the current computing component of the curriculum in civil engineering.

本文呈现了由……所实施的……调查结果。

例 2 **The paper provides a brief history of** scenario planning as it emerged from business-strategic planning activities and gives an overview of its goals and limitations. **The paper then reviews the context for** scenario-planning in regional transportation planning as well as precedents of its application in this field.

本文先简要回顾了……的历史。接着，本文回顾了……的背景。

2. 必要性、重要性（见表 2-3）

表 2-3 必要性、重要性的写作范式

This analysis/article/essay paper/thesis	considers/ deems it necessary to...	本文认为……是必要的
It	is necessary to...	本文认为……十分有必要
...	create(s) new problems and call(s) for new...	……提出了新问题，需要新的……
	has (have) resulted in a need for...	……导致了对于……的需求
	require(s) an effective...	……需要行之有效的……
	is an essential process to...	……是……的重要环节
	play(s) important roles in...	……在……中起着重要的作用
	is an important means of...	……的重要途径
	will be important	……将会至关重要

参见下例：

例 1 Wireless networks combined with location technology **create new problems and**

call for new decision aid.

……提出了新问题,需要新的……

例2　Scale structure and composition **play important roles in** the reactions of iron scales that lead to iron release, and water quality control to decrease the porosity of the scale **is an important means of** reducing iron release.

……起着重要的作用,……是……的重要途径。

例3　Rapid prototyping and development of in-circuit and FPGA-based emulators as key accelerators for fast time-to-market **has resulted in a need for** efficient error correction mechanisms. Fabricated or emulated prototypes upon error diagnosis **require an effective** engineering change (EC).

……导致了对于……的需求。……需要行之有效的……

例4　Consultant's pre-selection **is an essential process to** distinguish capable candidates before they are invited to submit their technical and free proposals for consultancy assignments.

……是……的重要环节。

例5　Limiting strip commercial development, establishing urban growth boundaries, and keying future office development to areas with good transit service **will be important**.

……将会至关重要。

例6　When construction delays occur, **it is necessary to** ascertain the liabilities of the contracting parties and to direct the appropriate amount of resources to recover the schedule. **Unfortunately**, delays and schedule compression are normally treated as separate or independent aspects.

……十分有必要。遗憾的是,……

3. 局限性(见表2-4)

表2-4　局限性的写作范式

Previous surveys have addressed the question of… The surveys reported in this paper are a follow-up study to the earlier surveys.	先前所开展的调查研究探讨了……的问题;本文所述调查研究是对先前调查研究的后续跟进
Although this process has successfully achieved this objective, it is still not completely understood… there is limited information regarding … and no information could be found on the relationship between…and … To better understand …	尽管该过程成功实现了本目标,但是仍未完全明晰……有关……的信息依然十分有限;关于……与……之间的关系仍无稽可考。为了更好地理解……
The limitations of…are discussed.	对于……(研究的)局限性做了论述……
… has the potential to … However, no comparative studies on… are available, and… has not been attempted.	仍有潜在可能……然而,在……方面尚无同类研究可供参考;对……也未予以尝试
…is a major contributor to… however it is much neglected in the research and planning activities of…	……对于……是一个巨大的贡献;然而,在……的研究和规划中,仍有诸多因素被疏漏
Despite the recent…of	尽管最近的……

参见下例：

例1 **Previous surveys completed** in 1989 and 1995 **have addressed the question of** what should be taught to civil engineering regarding computing. **The surveys reported in this paper are a follow-up study to the earlier surveys.**

先前所开展的调查研究探讨了……的问题；本文所述的调查研究是对先前调查研究的后续跟进。

例2 **The limitations of** such modeling also **are discussed**…

本文对……的局限性进行了论述。

例3 This distribution of freight **is a major contributor to** the levels of traffic congestion in cities. **However, it is much neglected in the research and planning activities of** government, where the focus is disproportionately on passenger vehicle movements. **Despite the recent** recognition of the performance of contribution of freight transportation to the performance of urban areas under the rubric of city logistics, **we see a void in the study** how the stakeholders in the supply chain might cooperate through participation in distribution networks, to reduce the costs associated with traffic congestion.

……对于……是一个巨大的贡献；然而，在……的研究和规划中，仍有诸多因素被疏漏。尽管最近的……，笔者在研究中发现依然有一空缺……

例4 The trickling filter/solids contact (TF/SC) process was developed in the late 1970s to improve the quality of the final effluent from existing trickling filter plants, **to be able to meet stricter** Environmental Protection Agency effluent **requirements. Although this process has successfully achieved this objective,** it is still not completely understood, **there is limited information regarding** the flocculation phenomena occurring in the solids contact chamber (SCC), **and no information could be found on the relationship between** flocculation **and** organic matter removal kinetics. **To better understand**…

……为能满足更为严格的……要求。尽管该过程成功实现了本目标，但是仍未完全明晰……；有关……的信息依然十分有限；关于……与……之间的关系仍无稽可考。为了更好地理解……

例5 **Several writers have reported that** this irrigation system **has the potential to** conserve water as compared to level-basin irrigation. **However, no comparative studies on** the performance of both irrigation systems **are available, and** the stimulation of level furrows **has not been attempted. In this work,** two field experiments are reported…

据先前多位研究人员所述，……仍有潜在可能……；然而，在……方面尚无同类研究可供参考；对……也未予以尝试。在本研究中……

2.3.3 研究目的的写作范式

研究目的即对该研究要达到的目的进行陈述。介绍论文研究目的时常用到的表达范式如表2-5所示。

表 2-5 研究目的的写作范式

This analysis/article/essay/paper/thesis	aims to…	本文旨在……
	attempts to …	
	makes an attempt to…	
	tries to…	本文力图……
	intends to…	
	is intended to…	
The chief/key/main/major/primary/principal aim/attempt/goal/object/objective/proposal/purpose of this paper/research/work	is to…	本文的主要目的是……
To/In order to…	assess/evaluate	为了评估……
	compare	为了比较……
	clarify	为了厘清……
	describe	为了描述……
	determine	为了确定……
	explore	为了探求……
	examine/testify/check	为了验证……
	identify	为了鉴定……
	improve	为了改进……
	investigate	为了调查……
	study	为了研究……
To this end	… is (was) studied	为此目的……研究了……
In this paper	we wish to…	在本论文中,作者意在……

参见下例:

例1 **The primary objectives of the investigation are to** assess the bridge's loading-carry capacity and compare this capacity with current standard of safety.

本调查研究的主要目的是……

例2 **The aim of this paper is to** devise a more objective framework for evaluating consultants' general capabilities during the pre-selection process.

本文旨在……

例3 **The aim of this article is to** determine with real data to what extent the hypotheses on which Clement's first formula is based are fulfilled, and to compare the results of applying this formula.

本文旨在……

例4 **To this end** the flow demand in the peak period **was studied** in two distribution networks with different irrigation methods and crops located in the Ebro River basin (northeast Spain).

为此目的……研究了……

例5 **To better understand** the kinetics of biological flocculation in a continuous flow SCC, a long-term experimental program was conducted using a TF/SC pilot plant constructed at the Marrero, La, wastewater treatment plant.

为更好地理解……

例 6 **The purpose of this paper is to** examine critically the implications of the new categories and paradigm shift in light of the main purpose protected areas, to protect wild biodiversity.

本文的研究目的是……

2.3.4 研究方法的写作范式

研究方法即对研究过程中所采用的技术、手段、方法以及工具、器械、仪表等进行简要说明，有时也应对所采用的原理、定律予以简明扼要的描述。介绍论文研究方法时常用到的表达范式如下。

1. 研究方法与原理（见表 2-6）

表 2-6 研究方法与原理的写作范式

A…based …is used, which requires…	使用了基于……的……，该……要求……
A…model is developed to represent…	研发了……模式，用以呈现……
A… model tested the …of…	……模型检测了……
A simple modification in the model changes the focus from …to …	对模型的简单调整使得重点从……变为……
A…system was used to …	……系统用以……
…was(were) treated with…	用……处理了……
…measurements were made…	测定了……
…were randomly divided/grouped into…groups	……被随机分成……组
…were separated into…groups based on…	基于……将……分成……组
Statistical methods… was used for…	使用……数据统计方法来……
… also incorporates a…	……结合……
The new… system has been tested in…	新的……系统在……得以验证
The proposed… employs an information system to store…	所提议的……采用信息系统来存储……
The samples of… were collected by…	……的样本由……收集
The test for…has been carried out…	对……的测试由……实施
We sampled the… of…	笔者对……进行了取样
We experimented on the property of…	笔者对于……的属性进行了试验
Using…(technique), we studied…	笔者用……（技术）研究了……
Using…, it was found that…	（笔者）用……发现了……
…was(were) measured using…	（笔者）用……测定了……
By performing a one-dimensional analysis on a…	通过对……的一元分析
With reference to…,…is obtained, … problem is solved through … method.	参照……，获取……，难题通过……方法予以解决
In order to examine the…, a questionnaire survey has been conducted with…	为验明……，（笔者）实施了……的问卷调查方式

参见下例：

例 1 Dynamic-**based** evaluation **is used**, **which requires** combining finite-element bridge analysis and field testing. **A** 3D finite-element **model is developed to** represent the bridge and to establish its deformed equilibrium configuration due to dead loading.

使用了基于……的……,该……要求……。研发了……模型,用以……

例 2 **To better understand** the kinetics of biological flocculation in a continuous flow SCC, **a long-term experimental program was conducted using** a TF/SC pilot plant constructed at the Marrero, La, wastewater treatment plant.

采用……,实施了一项长期实验项目,旨在更好地理解……

例 3 The proposed scheduling model (DSM) **employs an information system to store data** related to various work sites, activities' optional construction methods, and available resources. The DSM **also incorporates** a scheduling **algorithm** that is resource focused, and maintains crew work continuity under any sequence of distributed sites. **To minimize cost and meet project time and resource constraints**, the DSM **uses** genetic **algorithm to** determine the optimum set of construction methods and optimum routing order among sites.

……采用信息系统来存储数据。……还结合了……算法。为降低造价,不误工期,节约资源,……采用……算法来……

例 4 **In order to examine the importance of** pre-selection criteria, **a questionnaire survey has been conducted with clients** who are responsible for pre-selecting their consultants; and consultants being pre-selected by the clients.

为检验……的重要性,向客户实施了问卷调查……

例 5 **By performing a one-dimensional analysis on** a steady nonuniform flow through the weir, discharge is described as a function of related parameters, such as flow depth on the top-and-downstream sides of the weir, porosity, and grain diameter of the rubble mound, weir length, etc.

通过对……开展一元分析法……

例 6 **A simple modification in the model changes the focus from** minimizing total cost **to** minimizing project completion time subject to a resource constraint.

对模型的简单调整使得重点从……变为……

例 7 A geographic information **system was used to** assemble these data. **A logit regression model tested the significance of** geographic **variables** such as proximity to highway projects, land-use zoning classification, city size, and other spatial characteristics.

……系统用以……。……模型测试了……变量的重要性。

例 8 **The specimens were observed to** dilate under compressive stresses and the deformation behavior was seen to be dependent on the hydrostatic as well as the deviatoric stresses.

观察了……样(标)本,……

2. 研究数据的测量与计算(见表 2-7)

表 2-7 研究数据的测量与计算的写作范式

The average…increases with…	平均……随……增长
The mean percent differences between… and … that were observed indicated that… and it was evident that…	所观测到的……与……的平均值百分差显示……,且清楚表明……

续表

The author has computed/worked out…	笔者计算了……
In this paper, we measured…	笔者测量了……
Comparing…and…it was found that…	通过将……与……进行对比,发现……
The…range of…was measured by…	……测量了……的范围
The…rate of…was calculated by means of…	通过……方式计算了……的比率
The…was estimated…	对……进行了估算

参见下例:

例 1 **The test results indicate** stiffness **increases of over** 200% **and** strength **gains of over** 60% relative to the expected response of a noncomposite girder.

测试数据表明……增长了……,同时……增加了……

例 2 An upper bond **is calculated** for the steady-state deformation rates within a plane strain half space comprising the idealized asphalt mix subject to a uniform pressure over a finite contact strip.

计算了……

2.3.5 研究结果的写作范式

研究结果即对研究所获得的实验数据、实验现象、实验结果或推理得到的理论结果进行简要描述。介绍论文研究结果时常用到的表达范式如表 2-8 所示。

表 2-8 研究结果的写作范式

It is found that…	(结果)发现……
The…are found to be…	
…is confirmed	(结果)证实……
…demonstrate	(结果)显示……
…showed…	
Key findings of the study include…	该研究的主要发现包括……

参见下例:

例 1 **It is demonstrated that** cable stress stiffening **plays an important role in** both the static and dynamic response of the bridge. Inclusion of large deflection behavior **is shown to have a limited effect on** the member forces and bridge deflections.

(结果)显示……对……起重要作用,……对……的作用有限。

例 2 Measured flexural strains **showed** a strain discontinuity at the glulam-concrete interface **as expected**.

与预期一致,……显示……

例 3 The average oxidation state of iron **increases with** distance from the pipe wall. Scale structure and composition **play important roles in the reactions of** iron scales that lead to iron release, and water quality control to decrease the porosity of the scale **is an**

important means of reducing iron release.

……随……而增加。……在……反应中起重要作用。……是……的重要途径。

例 4 **Analysis of** wastewater composition **revealed that**, on the average, only 18.7% of the total COD in the SCC influent is truly dissolved. **Therefore**, most of the total COD removal observed in the SCC **must be due to** a physical process, such as flocculation.

……分析显示……。因此,……可能归因于……

例 5 **With reference to** a Logit path choice model, an implicit path enumeration network loading procedure **is obtained as an extension of** Dial's algorithm; the fixed-point **problem is solved through** the Bather's method.

根据……,获取了……以作为对……的延伸(扩充);通过……方法,得以解决……问题。

例 6 **Key findings of the study include**:(1) the relative importance of the top four skills (spreadsheets, word processors, computer-aid design, electric communication) has remained unchanged;(2) programming competence is ranked very low by practitioners;(3) the importance and use of geographic information system and specialized engineering software have increased over the past decade;(4) the importance and use of expert system have significantly decreased over the past decade;(5) the importance and use of equation solvers and databases have declined over the past decade.

该研究的主要发现包括……

2.3.6 研究结论的写作范式

研究结论即对研究成果所蕴含的意义、用途,以及该研究与其他同类研究之间的关系进行概述。介绍论文研究所得结论时常用到如下表达范式。

1. 研究结论(见表 2-9)

表 2-9 研究结论的写作范式

The study of... indicates/reveals/shows/suggests that...	该研究表明……
The authors conclude that...	归根结底,笔者认为……

参见下例:

例 1 **The findings reveal that** the perception of the client and consulting groups on the importance of CPC was very consistent.

该研究表明……

例 2 **The authors conclude that** anticipating congestion problems early combined with a "dare-to-do" attitude have resulted in being able to sustain a high level of service despite Singapore's compact size and rapid economic growth.

归根结底,笔者认为……

2. 用途启示(见表2-10)

表2-10 用途启示的写作范式

The approach can be used with…	该方法可用以……
Based on…,…can determine…	基于……,……可决定……
The model can be used for answering various "what if" questions that may be very helpful to…	该模式可用以回答各种"如果……怎么办"之类的问题,该类问题有助于……
The outcome of the investigation is to provide…	该调查的结果定将为……提供……
It is anticipated that the conceptual model presented here will be used as a basis for…	可以预计,本文所提出的概念模式将作为……的根据
Overall, the results suggest improvements to…	总之,研究结果表明在……方面的诸多改进
Significant improvements in performance appear possible through…	通过……,有望在性能方面取得巨大的改进
The present study makes it possible to apply…	当前研究使得运用……成为可能
These models provide a viable alternative to…	该模型为……提供了一个可供实现的替代方案
The model was implemented to predict…when…	该模式用以预测当……时……
Model results also suggests benefits for…	模型结果表明对……同样有益
The results of… effort illustrate the value of…	……努力的结果表明了……的价值所在

参见下例:

例1 **The approach can be used with** non-convace fundamental diagrams and multiple bottlenecks, even if they pass each other.

该方法可用以……

例2 **The outcome of the investigation is to provide** structural **information that will assist** the preservation of the historic John A. Roebling suspension bridge, though the developed methodology could be applied to a wide range of cable-supported bridges.

该调查的结果定将为……提供……信息,该信息将有助于……

例3 **Based on** each candidate score, clients **can determine** which engineering consultants should be invited to bid for a consultancy assignment.

基于……,……可决定……

例4 **The present study makes it possible to apply** the rubble mound weir for practical use as a discharge control system.

当前研究使得运用……成为可能。

例5 **The model can be used for answering various "what if" questions that may be very helpful to** a project manager in making rational decisions. **These models provide a viable alternative to more specialized** algorithms developed for the time/cost trade-off problem simply because a typical project manager may not have the necessary skills or resources to implement specialized algorithms.

该模式可用以回答各种"如果……怎么办"之类的问题,该类问题有助于……。该模型为……提供了一个可供实现的替代方案。

例 6 **It is anticipated that the conceptual model presented here will be used as a basis for** changing water quality to minimize colored water formation, and as a guide for further research.

可以预计,本文所提出的概念模式将作为……的根据。

例 7 **Overall, the results suggest improvements to** system operation and water allocations with a statewide expected value potentially as high as \$1.3 billion/year. **Significant improvements in performance appear possible through** water transfer and exchanges, conjunctive use, and various operational changes to increase flexibility. **These changes also greatly reduce costs to** agricultural and urban users of accommodating environmental requirements. **Model results also suggest benefits for** expanding selected conveyance **and** storage facilities.

总之,研究结果表明了在……方面的诸多改进。通过……,有望在性能方面取得巨大的改进。该变化同样大大降低了……的造价。模型结果表明对……同样有益。

例 8 **The results can be used for** the optimizing allocation of resources for road maintenance and rehabilitation.

其结果可用以……

例 9 **The results of this 4-year effort illustrate the value of** optimization modeling for providing integrated information needed to manage a complex multipurpose water system.

4 年辛勤努力的结果表明了……的价值所在。

3. 后续研究(见表 2-11)

表 2-11　后续研究的写作范式

… will call for new forms of…, greater supporter of…	……需要新式的……,需要更多的……支撑
Although there is already…, more… is still needed.	尽管已经……,仍然亟需更多的……

参见下例:

例 1 Maintaining future livability **will call for new forms of** metropolitan governance, **greater supporter of** transportation…

……需要新式的……,需要更多的……支撑。

例 2 We believe this approach opens the way to further development on problems in H-minor-free graphs.

笔者认为该方法为进一步探究有关……方面的问题开辟了一条途径。

2.3.7　范文分析

本节选出两篇英文学术论文的摘要全文,通过分析范文可以清晰地看到学术论文摘要的结构特征和语言特征。

1. 范文一

Abstract

（1）**This paper presents** the problem definition and guidelines of a set of benchmark control problems for seismically excited nonlinear buildings.（2）Focusing on three typical steel structures，3-，9-，and 20-story buildings designed for the SAC project for the Los Angeles，California region，**the goal of this study is to provide a clear basis to** evaluate the efficacy of various structural control strategies.（3）A nonlinear **evaluation model has been developed** that portrays the salient features of the structural system.（4）**Evaluation criteria and control constraints are presented** for the design problems.（5）**The task** of each participant in this benchmark study **is to define**（including sensors and control algorithms），**evaluate，and report** on their proposed control strategies.（6）**These strategies may be either passive，active，semiactive，or a combination thereof.**（7）The benchmark control problems **will then facilitate** direct comparison of the relative merits of the various control strategies.（8）To illustrate some of the design challenges，**a sample control strategy** employing active control with a linear quadratic Gaussian control algorithm **is applied** to the 20-story building.

（1）：研究主题

（2）：研究目的

（3）、(4)、(5)：
　　研究方法

（6）：研究结果
（7）：研究结论

（8）：研究方法

（*Journal of Engineering Mechanics*）

这篇摘要由 8 个句子构成，第 1 句交代了本论文研究的主要问题，第 2 句解释本研究的目的，第 3~5 句简要介绍本论文的研究方法，第 6 句为本研究的结果，第 7 句为本研究的结论及启示，第 8 句再次补充说明研究方法和手段。

2. 范文二

Abstract

（1）**This paper presents** the results of two surveys conducted by the American Society of Civil Engineers' Task Committee on Computing Education of the Technique Council on Computing and Information Technology **to assess** the current computing component of the curriculum in civil engineering.（2）**Previous surveys completed in** 1989 and 1995 **have addressed the question of** what should be taught to civil engineering regarding computing.（3）**The surveys reported in this paper are a**

（1）：研究主题
　　研究目的

（2）、(3)：
　　研究背景

follow-up study to the earlier surveys. (4) **Key findings of the study include**: the relative importance of the top four skills (spreadsheets, word processors, computer-aid design, electric communication) has remained unchanged; programming competence is ranked very low by practitioners; the importance and use of geographic information system and specialized engineering software have increased over the past decade; the importance and use of expert system have significantly decreased over the past decade; the importance and use of equation solvers and databases have declined over the past decade.

(4)：研究结果

(*Journal of computing in Civil Engineering*)

这篇摘要由4个句子构成，第1句交代了本论文的研究主题，兼论其研究目的，第2~3句简要回顾了本论文的相关研究背景以及本研究与先前研究的关系，第4句详细罗列了本论文的研究结果。

研究主题、研究背景、研究目的、研究方法、研究结果、研究结论六个要素通常是论文摘要中必须呈现的内容，是摘要写作中不可或缺的要素。事实上，摘要写作中除上述不可或缺的要素外，还有一些要素属于选择性要素，如研究范围、结果论证等，是否在摘要中出现，可视具体研究的特点和性质而定。

2.4 练习题

1. 英语学术论文摘要大体包含哪些构成要素？
2. 按照学术论文摘要的篇章构成要素简要分析下面这篇摘要。

Abstract

Consultants pre-selection is an essential process to distinguish capable candidates before they are invited to submit their technical and free proposals for consultancy assignments. Despite that, many clients have their own criteria and emphasis, and this could result in discrepancies in pre-selection decisions. The aim of this paper is to devise a more objective framework for evaluating consultants' general capabilities during the pre-selection process. The paper begins by identifying the commonly used criteria for pre-selecting engineering consultants. In order to examine the importance of pre-selection criteria (CPC), a questionnaire survey has been conducted with clients who are responsible for pre-selecting their consultants; and consultants being pre-selected by the clients. The findings reveal that the perception of the client and consulting groups on the importance of CPC was very consistent. Finally, a multi-criteria model for evaluating consultants' general capabilities during the pre-selection is proposed. Based on each candidate score, clients can determine which engineering consultants should be invited to bid for a consultancy assignment.

(Engineering, Construction and Architectural Management)

3. 将下面这篇摘要的各部分重新排序,使其符合英语摘要的写作规范。

A. Although this process has successfully achieved this objective, it is still not completely understood, there is limited information regarding the flocculation phenomena occurring in the solids contact chamber (SCC), and no information could be found on the relationship between flocculation and organic matter removal kinetics.

B. The trickling filter/solidscontact (TF/SC) process was developed in the late 1970s to improve the quality of the final effluent from existing trickling filter plants, to be able to meet stricter Environmental Protection Agency effluent requirements.

C. This program started in January 1998 and has continued through date.

D. The present article will focus on twomajorareas: (1) the kinetics of bioflocculation in the SCC; and (2) effect of bioflocculation on chemical oxygen demand (COD) removal.

E. To better understand the kinetics of biological flocculation in a continuous flow SCC, a long-term experimental program was conducted using a TF/SC pilot plant constructed at the Marrero, La, wastewater treatment plant.

F. Therefore, most of the total COD removal observed in the SCC must be due to a physical process, such as flocculation.

G. The experimental data confirmed that flocculation of the participate COD contained in the trickling filter effluent explains the high total COD removal observed at the SCC.

H. Analysis of wastewater composition revealed that, on the average, only 18.7% of the total COD in the SCC influent is truly dissolved.

I. Both total and colloidal COD removals are well explained by the first-order flocculation model.

(Journal of Environmental Engineering)

4. 阅读下面三篇摘要,说明它们从功能上分别属于哪种类型。

I

This first part of a two-part paper on the John A. Roebling suspension bridge (1867) across the Ohio River is an analytic investigation, whereas Part II focuses on the experimental investigation of the bridge. The primary objectives of the investigation are to assess the bridge's loading-carry capacity and compare this capacity with current standard of safety. Dynamic-based evaluation is used, which requires combining finite-element bridge analysis and field testing. A 3D finite-element model is developed to represent the bridge and to establish its deformed equilibrium configuration due to dead loading. Starting from the deformed configuration, a model analysis is performed to provide the frequencies and mode shapes. Transverse vibration modes dominate the low-frequency response. It is demonstrated that cable stress stiffening plays an important role in both the static and dynamic response of the bridge. Inclusion of large deflection behavior is shown to have a limited effect on the member forces and bridge deflections. Parametric studies are performed using the developed finite-element model. The outcome of the investigation is to provide structural information that will assist the preservation of the historic John A. Roebling suspension bridge, though the developed methodology could be applied to a wide range of cable-supported bridges.

(*Journal of Bridge Engineering*)

II

The aim of this article is to determine with real data to what extent the hypotheses on which Clement's first formula is based are fulfilled, and to compare the results of applying this formula. To this end the flow demand in the peak period was studied in two distribution networks with different irrigation methods and crops located in the Ebro River basin (northeast Spain). The calibration procedure for this formula proposed by the Center Technique du Genie Rural des Eaux et des Forest (CTGREF) in 1977 was also analyzed. The result was that most of the hypotheses were not fulfilled. Furthermore, the discharge distributions obtained in the period of study did not correspond to a normal distribution. However, comparing the real accumulated probability curve and that calculated by Clement's formula, it was found that the differences between the two curves for probabilities greater than 90% (a wide range of application of the formula) were lower than 9.4%. The reason for this result was found. It was shown also, that the CTGREF adjustment procedure did not provide substantial improvement in the estimation of flows because the aim of the fit was to achieve a normal distribution rather than an accumulated distribution function.

(*Journal of Irrigation and Drainage Engineering*)

III

Singapore has a world-wide reputation for efficiency and this extends to both its transport demand management and its excellent public transport service. In this paper, the authors look back at the early planning decisions which created the environment within which the current systems could develop. Increasingly, intelligent transport systems are being deployed and the current emphasis is on integrating these systems so that they work synergistically. The authors conclude that anticipating congestion problems early combined with a "dare-to-do" attitude have resulted in being able to sustain a high level of service despite Singapore's compact size and rapid economic growth.

(*Traffic Engineering & Control*)

5. 简要分析下面两篇摘要的人称、时态和语态。

I

This paper presents a flexible mixed integer-programming model for the solution of the time /cost trade-off problem encountered in project management. Whereas it is commonly assumed that the time/cost function is linear, the model presented in this paper makes minimal assumptions and accommodates any type of cost function is linear, piecewise linear or discrete. The model can be used for answering various "what if" questions that may be very helpful to a project manager in making rational decisions. The basic model minimizes the total cost which is the sum of direct or indirect costs, subject to a project deadline constraint. A simple modification in the model changes the focus from minimizing total cost to minimizing project completion time subject to a resource constraint. The models of this paper can be set up and run very easily on commercially optimization packages with an integer-programming module. These models provide a viable alternative to more specialized algorithms developed for the time/cost trade-off problem simply because a typical project manager may not have the necessary skills or resources to implement specialized algorithms.

(*Journal of Construction Engineering and Management*)

II

This analysis examines the historical relationship between land-use and the location of capacity-increasing highway projects in Oregon from 1970 to 1990. Aerial photography for 15 cities was used to delineate the extent of urban development for the 20-year time period. A geographic information system was used to assemble these data. A logit regression model tested the significance of geographic variables such as proximity to highway projects, land-use zoning classification, city size, and other spatial characteristics. The results suggest that for the 15 selected cities, the spatial measures performed well in predicting the location of urban development from 1970 to 1990. In addition, the results of logit regression model indicate that, controlling for other location factors, urban development impacts near state highway project corridors have produced a significant gradient of land-use change compared to the gradient for all highway facilities.

(*Journal of Urban Planning and Development*)

6. 用表中所给词的正确形式填空，注意时态和语态。

| be in general agreement with | calculate | conduct |
| observe | present | see to agree well with |

Abstract

A micromechanical model for the steady-state deformation of idealized asphalt mixes ____1____. Triaxial compression tests ____2____ on idealized asphalt mixes and the volumetric and deviatoric strains measured. The specimens ____3____ to dilate under compressive stresses and the deformation behavior was seen to be dependent on the hydrostatic as well as the deviatoric stresses. A simple model for the nonlinear viscous steady-state behavior of idealized mixes is presented based on a "shear box" analogy. Predictions of the model ____4____ experimental measurements for a wide range of conditions. An upper bond ____5____ for the steady-state deformation rates within a plane strain half space comprising the idealized asphalt mix subject to a uniform pressure over a finite contact strip. The deformation rate varies nonlinearly with the applied load and is strongly dependent on the hydrostatic stress. Further, the deformation rate is seen to be a maximum at a position about half a contact length below the surface of the half space. These findings ____6____ wheel tracking experiments on these idealized mixes.

(*Journal of Materials in Civil Engineering*)

7. 试析下面两篇摘要在研究主题、研究背景、研究目的等要素的提出以及表述方面的异同。

I

America's highways have developed dramatically over the last century, evolving into an extensive system of interconnected motorways. Lessons learned during this evolution suggest some future directions and challenges. Since 1916, cooperative federal-state partnerships and funding arrangements have evolved, continually broadening in scope to address new challenges, including environmental and urban concerns. As in the past, more people driving more cars and occupying more land will necessitate better roads and improved public transport. While land use and traffic management policies might reduce demands for highways, they will not substitute for needed investments. While there will be more high-occupancy vehicle toll (HOT) lanes, it will still be necessary to complete missing road links and to alleviate major bottlenecks.

(*Journal of Transportation Engineering*)

II

With the developing of city's economy and the increasing city problems, and accompanied with the course of Beijing's new period of urban construction, Beijing's urban-rapid rail transit(URRT) is going to develop very fast in the coming few years. With the rapid expansion of Beijing URRT web, the method of widely traveling by URRT will bring enormous influence on people's living, which will apply new changes for the layout of both urban spaces and the URRT web. The paper based on analysis the particularity of URRT traveling and the developing of Beijing URRT, combine with the analysis of diverse development and the multi-connection requirements, by examine the time consumption and capacity of Beijing URRT system, discovered that connection of urban spaces and Beijing URRT should be enhanced to fit for current metropolitan people's humanity living. In order to comply with humanity developing standard, the idea that URRT and urban spaces must integrate to fit for urban multi-service requirement is brought out by combination with the URRT system and urban spaces integrate-developing. In order to control total commuting time and assign it reasonably in several aspect, by analysis the related aspects and the reasonable time that can be allotted in the three levels of urban system such as node, route and web in the course of people's commuting, and also judged from multi-developing and multi-connection requirements of the city's layout, the principles of improving the structure and controlling the developing range of urban development areas is given to the three levels of urban spaces. And also some principles of the adjustment on the functions, capacities and the form of the related urban spaces and URRT system are drawn out. Illustrated from some good examples of URRT integrate developing with urban spaces of some developed cities of world, the methods of urban spaces integrated with URRT is discussed separately in the three levels of spaces after analyzing current conditions of Beijing urban spaces and URRT. Some particular ways to integrate Beijing urban spaces with the URRT system are put forward to give references and advices on how to realize a sustainable developing of urban spaces and the URRT in Beijing's complex metropolitan system of city transportation, city living and city construction.

(http：//www.cnki.net/kcms/detail/detail.aspx? dbcode＝cdfd&queryid＝3&currec＝59&dbname＝cdfdlast2011&filename＝2010214902.nh&uid＝weevredisutucelbv1vfq2nsa0dncta3m3qzzwn1bfcrana1nzlta1pzs0nhtdnyk1k0ni93umjyewtztdfvpq＝＝)

2.5 相关阅读

1. Supplementary Reading Material 1

Types of Abstracts

Many different labels are used to describe abstracts. Among them are critical abstracts, slanted abstracts, and highlight abstracts, as well as the more typical informative and descriptive abstracts.

Critical abstracts are unusual but have some attractions for the user. A well-produced critical abstract not only describes the document content, but also evaluates the work and its presentation. A critical abstract normally indicates the depth and extent of the work, commenting on the appropriateness of the work for the intended audience, and the significance of the contribution to the development of knowledge. The preparation of a critical abstract not only requires first class abstracting skills but also a subject knowledge which extends beyond a mere understanding, to a full appreciation of the relative significance of various contributions. The abstractor injects his or her opinions and analysis.

Slanted abstracts may be informative, descriptive, or critical abstracts that have been oriented towards the interests of a known audience. Such abstracts are particularly attractive to the audience for whom they have been drafted. For instance, if the intended audience is a chain of travel agents who specialize in nature trips for hikers and campers, the abstractor will seek any reference to natural attractions, in particular parks, forests, hiking trails, camp grounds or other outdoor recreational sites. Even where natural attractions only feature as a minor aspect of the document content or as a side issue, an abstract slanted towards the chain of travel agents might dwell almost entirely upon the information concerning outdoor possibilities.

Highlight abstracts are designed to attract the reader's attention to an article and to whet the appetite. No pretence is made of their being either a balanced or complete picture of the article. Indeed to spark readers' curiosity incomplete and leading remarks are possibly the most effective. In that a highlight abstract cannot stand independent of its associated article, it is not a true abstract.

Informative and *descriptive abstracts* are certainly the most common types of abstracts; in fact many people feel that they are the only types of abstracts that can be regarded as true abstracts. Informative abstracts present as much as possible of the quantitative or qualitative information contained in a document. This satisfies twin objectives. Informative abstracts both aid in the assessment of document relevance and selection or rejection, and act as a substitute for the document when a superficial or outline knowledge of document content is satisfactory. An informative abstract presents a clear condensation of the essential arguments and findings of the original. Descriptive abstracts merely indicate the content of an article and contain general statements about the document—no attempt is made to report the actual content of the article as in informative abstracts. Descriptive abstracts abound in phrases such as "is discussed" or "are dealt with," yet do not record the outcome of the discussions. Thus, a descriptive abstract is no more than a sophisticated selection aid. Since the treatment is more superficial than in an informative abstract, the descriptive abstract can be written quickly and economically and requires less perception and subject expertise on the part of the abstractor than an informative abstract. A descriptive abstract is not intended to act as a document substitute in the true sense, so its application and value are more limited than those of an informative abstract, and, cost considerations aside, an informative abstract is to be preferred in most instances.

Descriptive-informative abstracts are more common than either the pure *informative* or the pure *descriptive* abstract. Parts of the abstracts are written in the informative style, while those aspects of the document that are of minor significance are treated descriptively. Descriptive treatment may, in fact, be the only method of condensed presentation of document content in some cases: if, for example, the original document lists nine Civil Warbattlefield parks, purely informative treatment of this content would require the abstractor to list all nine parks by name, resulting in the same, or nearly the same length as the original. When used to good effect, this mixed style can achieve the maximum transmission of information, within the minimum length.

(*Abstracting and Indexing*)

2. Supplementary Reading Material 2
Journal Abstracts

Journal abstracts are usually requested by scholarly journals and written after the original manuscript was composed. While a proposal can be quite long depending on the assignment and purpose, an abstract is generally kept brief (approximately 150-200 words), but includes some of the same elements as a proposal:

- A statement of the problem and objectives
- A summary of employed methods or your research approach the significance of the proposed topic should become clear as well
- A self-contained piece of writing that can be understood independently from the essay or project

As journal editors still follow traditional criteria of clear argumentation, your journal abstract should include a valid thesis in understandable language and follow lucid, persuasive prose. Your first consideration should go towards a well thought out revision of the article you intend to submit for publication.

Rather than writing for your dissertation committee or professors, you will need to prove thorough comprehension of primary and secondary materials, and that you understand the positive and negative implications of these pieces of evidence.

You should learn about the specific journal audience, or the interested reader in the general public; thus, you should provide clear explanations of key terms and keep digressions to a minimum, preferably limited to the footnotes in the manuscript.

The abstract should tell readers whether they want to look at your article in more detail when reading it in the journal. Only a few journals ask you to send merely an abstract without a complete manuscript, and they mainly advertise these calls on their websites and general calls for papers websites of the various fields. English majors, for instance, may find a listing of these on the University of Pennsylvania English Department website.

Regardless of field, journal abstract authors should explain the purpose of the work, methods used, the results and the conclusions that can be drawn. However, each field purports slightly different ways to structure the abstract. Hartley and Sykes have suggested that papers for the social sciences (and any other empirical work) should contain the following:

- Background
- Aims
- Method
- Results
- Conclusions and comment

Most scientific journals require authors to submit such abstracts, whereas the social sciences and humanities journals do not always do so but are quickly catching up to the trend. It is generally advisable to write the abstract in the English language, as most papers in other languages, especially Asian nations, tend to publish an English abstract with common search engines, such as, the MLA site.

(https://owl.english.purdue.edu/owl/resource/752/04/)

3. Supplementary Reading Material 3
Planning, Developing and Writing an Effective Conference Abstract

John Albarran gives a step-by-step guide to ensuring the highest standards (and increasing the chance of acceptance) when preparing an abstract for submission.

In the past decade, the profession has witnessed a growth in the range of scientific conferences designed to meet the needs of general as well as specialist groups. This has stimulated a rise in the number of conference abstracts submitted by nurses wishing to disseminate aspects of their research or examples of innovation and good practice. As a result, the process of selecting abstracts is far more competitive and members of scientific panels have to make harsh decisions about which papers to accept and include in their conference programs. This development is clearly an indicator of a maturing research-based discipline. However, a successful abstract submission requires meticulous planning and developing a style of writing that is clear, succinct and informative. The aim of this paper is to review the essential stages of developing a strategy for writing a conference abstract that increases the chance of acceptance.

Introduction

Although the volume of abstract submissions led by nurses has increased, there is still much variation in standards. A lack of experience and inattention to detail during the writing stages are contributory factors. More usually, individuals will be unsuccessful when an abstract:

- Lacks stated aims and objectives
- Is unstructured, fragmented and lacking rigour
- Presents results in a vague and confusing manner
- Fails to convey the implications for the profession simply and succinctly
- Undersells—or oversells—the originality or uniqueness of the work

Condensing the results of a project or recently completed study concisely is challenging, yet crucial in ensuring an abstract meets the presentation standards of the scientific committee. The art of creating and writing a successful conference abstract is a skilled activity requiring attention to detail and an ability to write clearly, fluently and informatively. These skills can, however, be learned through practice and guidance.

The purpose of an abstract

An abstract is usually an "abstracted" short summary or synopsis of a larger piece of work that is prepared with a particular focus, aimed at a specific audience. Typically, a conference abstract is likely to be judged by a number of audiences for different purposes and this needs to be considered in the planning stages.

The first audience comprises experts who serve on the scientific panel of reviewers. Typically your abstract will be "blind" reviewed, often by a minimum of two members of the panel, according to set criteria. The abstract needs to persuade reviewers that the proposed work is of a high standard, sufficiently rigorous, makes a distinct contribution and supports the conference objectives. If the meeting has an international agenda, the relevance of the content to a wider global community will form part of the assessment. Therefore, it is important to integrate statements or references that stress international applicability as this will strengthen the standing of your abstract.

The second audience comprises conference delegates, who will assess accepted abstracts on whether the content is relevant to their work. The abstract outline will thus be influential in guiding delegates' decisions about which presentations to attend or posters to visit. Stimulating delegate interest will be largely dependent on the clarity and coherence of your abstract, the originality of ideas and application to practice.

A third but less obvious audience includes journalists. Media representatives (from the profession, national newspapers or regional television) may be covering a conference, and will scan the program handbook for newsworthy items. Abstracts thus provide primary sources of information and may lead to additional project exposure in the form of a news item. It may also lead to an approach from a journal editor, inviting you to develop a fuller paper for publication based on your poster or presentation. Additionally, to promote accessibility of work presented at conference, accepted abstracts in the form of "conference proceedings" may be published in journals linked with specific associations. It is thus vital that abstract layout and writing conventions are adhered to, as opportunities to edit or correct the text may not be possible before publication.

Starting with background work

For the majority of nurses, the decision to prepare an abstract will often be in response to a conference flyer or advert in a journal inviting submissions. Venue location can prove an incentive and prompt enthusiasm. In choosing which conference to submit an abstract to Coad et al. advise novice authors to target events that will not raise their discomfort levels, but will help develop their experience and expertise. It is therefore wise to read any information relating to the event carefully and visit the conference website. A number of issues will have a bearing on the writing stages.

What is the title and what are the conference themes?

Does the title suggest that the conference is appealing specifically to nurses in a specialist field of practice or aimed at a wider professional community? Are the themes broad enough to enable you to tailor an abstract to a specific topic area?

Ensuring that the content of an abstract complements and reflects the overall aims of the conference is vital to acceptance, as these aspects form part of the assessment criteria.

Who will be in the audience?

Identifying whether delegates represent a cross-section of the profession (practitioners, researchers, managers and educators) or come from a multidisciplinary background is important. Is the conference seeking to attract national and international delegates?

Thinking about these issues will make it possible to consider the choice of terms and writing style to adopt in the abstract. The use of language should be appropriate, inclusive and resonate with conference participants.

What is the format for an abstract? How, where and when to submit it?

Increasingly there is an expectation that potential contributors will submit their abstracts online.

Most events will provide a prescriptive set of guidelines for preparing an abstract (Table 1) but, as these may vary between conferences, ensure you have checked (and your abstract conforms to) the specific requirements in each case. For research-based papers, a structured abstract with standard headings will be required (background, aims, methods, results and discussion/conclusions). In others, a short paragraph that includes the aims and a list of learning outcomes for the presentation may be preferred. Failure to convey methodological clarity or conform to requirements may result in the abstract being declined. Reading and strictly following the instructions is vital at the writing stage.

Table 1 Typical list of instructions for preparing a conference abstract

List of authors, institutions and contact details
Contact details of corresponding author
Preference for presentation mode (oral or poster)
Title (must be short, not more than 12 words)
Structure of presentation (e.g., research)
List of learning outcomes (if applicable)
Word limit (often 200-300 words maximum)
Font size (not larger than 12 point)
Specified type of font (e.g., Times, Arial)
Specified number of references (maximum of three)
Specified referencing system (Vancouver or Harvard)
List of key words (maximum of four)
Declaration of any conflict of interests
Check whether tables/figures are permitted

The abstract may need to be E-mailed, uploaded or written directly into an online form. You may also need to decide whether to register for an oral or poster presentation at this stage. Some organizers request an abstract first and then decide on the required format for the presentation. The decision is not a reflection on the quality of the abstract.

The duration of oral presentations varies between conferences, lasting from 6-20 minutes. A degree of confidence with public speaking, dealing with audience questions and using audiovisual aids is required. In contrast, preparing an eye-catching, thought-provoking poster that engages delegates demands skill and creativity. There are usually specific instructions to follow regarding size and formatting.

Registering as a conference presenter and submitting an abstract is time-consuming. It is advisable to become familiar with this process, the guidelines for writing the abstract and the date for final submission. Following abstract registration, individuals will usually receive confirmation with a reference number for future correspondence.

Writing and shaping the abstract

Title

Over the years, it has become the vogue to have catchy and snappy titles. However, these can be very UK-centric and may not be understood by reviewers and delegates from abroad. The title should capture the essence of the content. If you are reporting the findings of research, it might be sensible to include the study design used. Posing a question within the title is also an effective strategy to prompt delegates' interest. Having a provocative statement as a title can work but a certain level of confidence may be required.

Main body

Because of the word limits imposed, it is important to be certain about the messages you wish to impart. Set time aside and decide on the aims, the structure and issues to be covered. Reflect on these aspects as well as on technical competence. An abstract that conveys a professional image will make a favourable impression with the target audiences.

For an abstract based on previous research, the use of standard headings is appropriate. If your work does not fall into this category, the abstract content must still be logically organized and systematic. In the case of a practice audit or literature review, the headings in Table 2 might be useful. Whatever approach you adopt for laying out the text, be sure to make the aims explicit.

Table 2 Suggested headings for non-research papers

Background/problem (state the nature and scope of the problem)
Aims/objectives of the presentation
Intervention (state what activities undertaken, on whom and by whom)
Results (describe the outcomes or changes in practice)
Discussion (what now? what are the implications for patient care, multidisciplinary working, bed-occupancy, waiting times, changing roles ...?)

Writing stages

Once the headings are agreed set about planning the balance of the text. A couple of sentences, underpinned by the literature, should be adequate to set the scene and theoretical background. Be concise and impress on the reader the nature of the problem and rationale for the project or enquiry. Methods or strategies employed to achieve your aim should then be briefly outlined. Haigh suggests that the inclusion of statistical data, where appropriate, may increase the chances of acceptance since it may be expected that the findings will fuel debate.

The areas needing most attention will be constructing a summary of the results and conclusions or implications for practice. Be economical with your choice of words—avoid squandering them by describing that the project formed part of a thesis, or saying who funded the study. With regard to references, be judicious and use those that demonstrate currency, appropriateness and focus on the topic.

There are other issues to be aware of when writing the abstract. It is good practice to leave out jargon, sound bites and colloquialisms as these may mean little to reviewers or conference participants from outside the UK. Some conferences may insist on omitting abbreviations or permit them, if written in full before use in the text.

In composing the content, use simple and standard terms that will communicate clearly with your reading public. Develop a writing style that is accessible and seek to enliven the text by deploying active verbs. Since the project you intend to present is historical, it is acceptable to write in the past tense, but take care not to mix your tenses. Importantly, avoid developing a pretentious and verbose literary style as this may obscure meaning and confuse readers. If available, obtain a sample of previously published abstracts so that you can gauge the approach and writing style used.

Improving the quality

Once you have completed the abstract, there are other additional steps necessary for improving the quality of the final draft. Planning for revisions and seeking feedback from peers are quality-control activities you can not ignore. An experienced critical friend can provide editorial advice and offer a constructive critique on your drafts, which will serve to raise the standard of your work. Give them plenty of time and do not expect immediate turn around.

Finally, to augment the appearance and image of the final abstract, Lindquist recommends attending to the three "Rs", namely reducing, refining and reviewing.

Reduction

Go through the document with a critical eye and remove redundant words. Edit long passages into shorter sentences. Use figures rather than words for numbers (e.g. 11 rather than eleven) and where possible discard irrelevant detail and repetitious text.

Refinement

Sharpen the focus of the abstract and make sure that key messages are implicit. To prepare an abstract that is clear, concise, logical and informative, use short words, delete ambiguous terms, jargon, superfluous statistics and P values. Amend and correct the abstract according to feedback. Undertake final touches, such as spacing, alignment of text, tenses and consistency in the use of language. Use gender-neutral terms and culturally sensitive language.

Review

At this stage, scrupulous proofreading is mandatory. Edit for grammar, punctuation, conformity, accuracy of data, spelling errors and appearance. With the advent of word-processing software, most of these problems are avoidable. In many cases, it is a failure to attend to these details that leads to rejection. The objective of the reviewing process should be on improving the readability, presentation style and scholarship of the abstract, and checking that it conforms to abstract standards laid down by the conference's scientific committee. These strategies are ultimately about placing your abstract in an optimal position and creating a positive and professional image. Finally, before submitting the abstract create a checklist to ensure you have addressed all requirements as laid out in the conference guidelines.

Conclusions

Writing an abstract for publication is a skilled art. For nurses to be successful in an increasingly competitive arena, they need to invest in forward planning, developing a strategy that ensures that their work is of an appropriate academic standard in keeping with the aspirations of the conference, and well presented. This paper has outlined some of the processes involved in the writing of a clearly informed, focused and cogent abstract. While it is recognized that there is no substitute for experience, the support of colleagues as "critical" readers and peers can play an important role in enabling inexperienced practitioners to gain confidence and competence in this area of professional practice.

(*British Journal of Cardiac Nursing*)

4. Supplementary Reading Material 4
How to Write an Abstract for Your Thesis or Dissertation

What is an Abstract?

- The abstract is an important component of your thesis. Presented at the beginning of the thesis, it is likely the first substantive description of your work read by an external examiner. You should view it as an opportunity to set accurate expectations.
- The abstract is a summary of the whole thesis. It presents all the major elements of your work in a highly condensed form.
- An abstract often functions, together with the thesis title, as a stand-alone text. Abstracts appear, absent the full text of the thesis, in bibliographic indexes such as PsycInfo. They may also be presented in announcements of the thesis examination. Most readers who encounter your abstract in a bibliographic database or receive an E-mail announcing your research presentation will never retrieve the full text or attend the presentation.
- An abstract is not merely an introduction in the sense of a preface, preamble, or advance organizer that prepares the reader for the thesis. In addition to that function, it must be capable of substituting for the whole thesis when there is insufficient time and space for the full text.

Size and Structure

- Currently, the maximum sizes for abstracts submitted to Canada's National

- Archive are 150 words (Master's thesis) and 350 words (Doctoral dissertation).
- To preserve visual coherence, you may wish to limit the abstract for your doctoral dissertation to one double-spaced page, about 280 words.
- The structure of the abstract should mirror the structure of the whole thesis, and should represent all its major elements.
- For example, if your thesis has five chapters (introduction, literature review, methodology, results, conclusion), there should be one or more sentences assigned to summarize each chapter.

Clearly Specify Your Research Questions
- As in the thesis itself, your research questions are critical in ensuring that the abstract is coherent and logically structured. They form the skeleton to which other elements adhere.
- They should be presented near the beginning of the abstract.
- There is only room for one to three questions. If there are more than three major research questions in your thesis, you should consider restructuring them by reducing some to subsidiary status.

Don't Forget the Results
- The most common error in abstracts is failure to present results.
- The primary function of your thesis (and by extension your abstract) is not to tell readers what you did, it is to tell them what you discovered. Other information, such as the account of your research methods, is needed mainly to back the claims you make about your results.
- Approximately the last half of the abstract should be dedicated to summarizing and interpreting your results.

(http://www.sfu.ca/~jcnesbit/HowToWriteAbstract.htm)

第3章 引言

3.1 概述

1. 引言的定义

引言也称为前言、序言、绪论、导论或概述,是一篇学术论文的开场白,目的是向读者说明当前研究的来龙去脉,简略描述论文内容或相关背景,吸引读者对论文的兴趣,对正文起到提纲挈领和引导阅读兴趣的作用。

2. 引言的作用和功能

作为论文的开头,引言需要以简短、凝练的篇幅介绍论文的写作背景、目的,提出研究的现实情况,以及相关领域内前人所做的工作和研究的概况,说明当前研究与前人研究的关系,目前的研究热点、存在的问题及当前研究的价值和意义,向读者引出论文的主题。引言也可以点明论文的理论依据、实验基础和研究方法,简单阐述研究内容,并预示本研究的结果、意义和前景,但不必展开讨论。引言的长短视论文内容和性质而定,涉及基础研究的学术论文的引言通常较长。大多国外期刊登载的学术论文引言较长,这与国外期刊约稿要求以及学术相关规范不无关系。

引言是为论文的写作立题,目的是引出下文。一篇论文只有"命题"成立,才有必要继续写下去,否则论文的写作就失去了意义。一般的学术论文引言包括两层意思:一是"立题"的背景,说明论文选题在本学科领域的地位、作用以及目前研究的现状,特别是前人研究中存在的或没有解决的问题;二是针对现有研究的状况,确立本文拟要解决的问题,从而引出下文。引言写作中要避免出现以下两方面的问题。

首先,文不着题,泛泛而谈。一些作者把论文的引言看成是一种形式,当作可有可无的部分,使引言的写作和正文的写作有剥离之感。常见的现象是,一般化地论述研究的重要性,缺乏与本研究的相关性,缺少对当前研究状况的概括和介绍。因而,读者无法准确地判断"论文命题"的具体价值,无法获知当前研究与以往的研究工作有什么不同。因此,学术论文的引言必须交代研究工作的背景,概括性地论述所研究问题的现状。对研究现状的论述,不仅考查作者对文献资料的掌握程度和熟悉程度,更重要的是,从资料的全面程度和新旧程度可以判断研究工作的意义和价值,同时说明研究结果的可信度。

其次,引文罗列,缺少分析和概括。引言不仅要反映研究背景的广度,更重要的是要考查作者对研究背景了解的深度。介绍研究现状的过程并非只是列出参考文献,需要拣选罗列出有代表性的、与当前研究有相关性的文献,也可以对相关研究者的不同做法和结论进行回顾。对前人研究的概述不可片面强调文献资料的丰富性，作者须对文献进行分析和归纳，概括出前人研究的成果和存在的问题。因此，在撰写引言之前，要尽可能多地了解前人研究的相关内容，收集前人研究工作的主要资料，从而能够有效说明本研究设想的合理性，同时呈现出当前研究的学术价值、实用价值或推广价值等。

3.2 构成要素

英文学术论文的引言通常由三部分构成：研究现状、研究中心及研究目的和意义。

1. 研究现状

研究现状即学术论文引言的起始部分。作者通过对研究现状的描述，说明当前研究的必要性和重要性，从而进一步突出该研究领域的意义和研究价值。研究现状通常包含以下构成要素：

要素1：背景信息；
要素2：相关研究领域的现状*；
要素3：研究的价值和重要性；
要素4：文献综述*。

在引言第一部分的四个要素中，并非所有的要素都应同时出现在一篇引言中。其中，标注*号的为必需性要素（obligatory elements），其他的为选择性要素（optional elements）。作者可以根据当前研究的特点、性质、对文献的掌握程度等方面的具体情况予以选择。

参见下例：

例1　Economic integration among economies of the world **has brought increased attention** of investors and academic scholars to the issue of interrelationships among these markets around the world.

……引发了广泛关注。（要素2：相关研究领域的现状）

例2　**There have been studies on** various factors that affect international market stock returns and variances.

就……有相关研究。（要素4：文献综述）

例3　**An important issue in** pattern recognition **is** the effect of insufficient samples available for training in classification accuracy.

……方面的重要问题是……（要素2：相关研究领域的现状）

例4　**Over a period of several decades**, wavelet analysis has been applied to quite diverse fields.

在过去的几十年间，……（要素1：背景信息）

例5　Insight into the behavior of pedestrians, and tools to predict this behavior, **are essential** in the planning and design of public pedestrian facilities such as airports, transfer stations, and shopping malls.

……对于……至关重要。（要素3：研究的价值和重要性）

例6　**Two general theories are available** to evaluate the cyclic loading behavior of structure：namely the isotropic and kinematic hardening theories.

对于……有两个普遍性理论。（要素4：文献综述）

例7 Considerable research has been carried out previously for the development of various techniques for bearing fault detection and diagnosis based on vibration.

对于……，前人进行了大量的研究。（要素4：文献综述）

虽然"背景信息"在引言的起始部分中并非必需性要素，但针对某些研究的特点和性质，追溯当前研究的历史和背景也是常见的开篇手段。并且，这也是中国学者在引言中较为多用的要素。

2. 研究中心

研究中心即学术论文引言的中间环节，在前人研究和当前研究的具体情况之间起衔接作用。在这一环节，作者可以指出前人研究的不足，或对前人研究提出质疑，也可以是在前人研究基础上继续进行研究。根据研究的具体特点和性质，可选择以下要素：

要素1：前人研究的不足；

要素2：提出须解决的问题；

要素3：继续前人的研究。

在这一环节的写作中，作者须根据自身研究的特点和性质选择其中任何一个要素作为具体的实现手段。其中，第一个要素是最常被选用的。

参见下例：

例1 **Although a number of authors have analyzed** the emergence of global competitors from developing countries, the phenomenon of M&A in the case of firms in developing countries, not as target firms but as acquiring ones, **has not been yet explicitly recognized.**

尽管很多学者对……进行了分析，但尚未明确确认……。（要素1：前人研究的不足）

例2 **While many studies analyze** stock returns around acquisitions, **few studies** consider changes in operating performance.

很多研究分析了……，对……的研究并不多见。（要素1：前人研究的不足）

例3 **However,** a geometrically linear theory **is not well adapted to** the design of suspension bridges with long spans, shallow trusses, or a large dead load. **A more exact theory is required** that takes into account the deformed configuration of the structure.

但是，……理论不适合于……，需要一个更为确切的理论对……（要素1：前人研究的不足）

例4 **The author's interest in this topic stems from** the report of a new mechanism for band gap formation in phononic crystals made of silicone-coated lead balls.

作者对于这一课题的兴趣源于……（要素3：继续前人的研究）

例5 **Very few** equilibrium data on this ligand **have been reported,** and the values of the equilibrium constants published differ greatly, even for identical systems.

对……研究尚不多见。（要素1：前人研究的不足）

例6 **However, few conservation scientists or conservationists seem to be aware of** the implications of the directions that have emerged regarding PA (protected areas) classification or the new paradigm.

然而，环保科学家和环保主义者似乎对……认识不足。（要素1：前人研究的不足）

例 7　The complexity of selecting efficient water management alternatives at both state and regional levels suggests that perhaps **a different, more integrated approach is needed to** complement existing simulation-based planning approaches.

需要一个不同的且更为综合的方法对现有的……进行补充。（要素 3：继续前人的研究）

例 8　**Although** there has been much interest in the design of new lanthanide selective ligands, **there have been few studies** of the thermodynamic stability of such complexes.

尽管……，但对于……的研究尚不多见。（要素 1：前人研究的不足）

例 9　The benchmark problem presented herein **is an extension of** the seismically excited next generation benchmark problem presented at the Second World Conference on Structural Control to include nonlinear responses and to address other building heights.

……是对……的延伸。（要素 3：继续前人的研究）

3. 研究的目的与意义

研究的目的与意义即陈述当前研究的目的和意义。学术论文引言的这一部分是对前文提到的不足予以解答。此外，也可对主要结果进行概括性描述。这个环节一般由以下几个要素构成：

要素 1：研究目的*；
要素 2：研究内容*；
要素 3：研究结果；
要素 4：用途启示及后续研究；
要素 5：结构框架。

在这一部分的五个具体实现要素中，也可以划分为必需性要素和选择性要素。要素 1 和要素 2 是必需性要素，其中要素 2 的写作内容可以包括当前研究的特点、性质、方法、价值、重要性及意义等。此外，作者可以根据当前研究的特点和性质等方面的具体情况对要素 3、要素 4 和要素 5 予以选择。要素 3 是针对研究结果的描述，因为出现在引言部分，通常只需对主要发现和结果进行概括性陈述，从而起到对结果予以佐证的目的。要素 4 的描述可以涵盖研究的局限、研究的启示、应用情况和前景以及未来的研究方向。要素 5 的选用取决于文章的篇幅、期刊约稿惯例及个人写作习惯，但大多数英文学术论文会介绍论文的结构框架，而结构框架在中文学术论文中较为罕见。

参见下例：

例 1　**Our aim, therefore, is to, first,** set out our analytical framework which we propose is driven by volatility and show how this might alter with the passage of time and, **second, to** provide evidence to indicate that option moneyness undermines the intended incentives put in place by option-based contracts.

当前的研究目的首先是……，其次是……（要素 1：研究目的）

例 2　**This paper is set up as follows. Section 2 describes** the empirical methodology. **Section 3 discusses** the data set and results, and **Section 4 presents** a brief conclusion.

本文结构如下，第二部分描述……，第三部分讨论……，第四部分呈现……（要素 5：结构框架）

例 3　**In this paper,** cyclic loading analysis of beams under different types of leading such as thermal, mechanical and their combinations **is investigated.**

本文调查了……（要素2：研究内容）

例4 **The primary objectives of the investigation are to assess** the bridge's load-carrying capacity and compare this capacity with current standards of safety.

当前研究的主要目标是对……进行评估。（要素1：研究目的）

例5 **Evaluation tests have confirmed** that the system that has been developed is even applicable to position detection in tunnels.

评估测试证实了……（要素3：研究结果【对结果予以佐证】）

例6 **The present research demonstrates** how one might identify the sensors and control devices employed, build a design model, develop a controller, and evaluate a complete control system design.

当前研究呈现了……（要素2：研究内容【揭示当前研究的价值、特点】）

例7 **The design offers** a simple and easily realizable way to solve sophisticated modern control problems.

这项设计提供了……（要素2：研究内容【揭示当前研究的价值】）

例8 **These models have been applied with success** to assist in the evaluation or optimization of designs of new or existing walking facilities.

这些模型已成功运用于……（要素4：用途启示）

例9 **The purpose of this paper is to** provide an international perspective to the dynamic relationship between the short-term nominal interest rate and the inflation rate.

本文的研究目的是……（要素1：研究目的）

例10 **This paper presents a quantitative description of** the dynamics of water quality variables monitored in influents and effluents during two consecutive growth cycles at four shrimp aquaculture farms.

本文是对……的定量描述。（要素2：研究内容【当前研究的性质、特点】）

引言作为学术论文的起始部分，须明确以下基本问题：(1)通过本论文说明什么问题；(2)有哪些新的发现；(3)是否有学术价值。读者读了引言以后，可以清楚地知道作者为什么选择该题目进行研究。为此，在撰写引言之前，要尽可能多地了解相关的内容，收集前人已进行工作的主要资料，说明本研究设想的合理性。在熟悉引言构成要素的基础上，进一步了解引言的基本话语特征是引言写作实践的重要环节。引言的构成要素如表3-1所示。

表3-1 引言的构成要素一览表

引言结构	结构要素	常用时态	说明
第一部分：研究现状	要素1：背景信息	一般现在时 一般过去时 现在完成时	
	要素2：相关研究领域的现状*	一般现在时	要素2和要素3可以合二为一
	要素3：研究的价值和重要性	一般现在时	
	要素4：文献综述*	一般现在时 一般过去时 现在完成时	

续表

引言结构	结构要素	常用时态	说明
第二部分：研究中心	要素1：前人研究的不足	一般现在时 现在完成时 一般过去时	引言多采用要素1
	要素2：提出须解决的问题	一般现在时	
	要素3：继续前人的研究	一般现在时	
第三部分：研究目的与意义	要素1：研究目的*	一般现在时	要素1和要素2可以合二为一
	要素2：研究内容*	一般现在时 一般过去时	
	要素3：研究结果	一般过去时 一般现在时	
	要素4：用途启示及后续研究	一般现在时	
	要素5：结构框架	一般现在时	

注：* 为引言必须涵盖的结构要素。

3.3 写作范式

学术论文引言的复杂性和特殊性决定了写作的难度。在撰写引言的过程中，须充分了解引言的话语特征和结构特征，同时，有必要遵循引言在句式、词汇和措辞等方面的写作范式。

3.3.1 研究现状的写作范式

引言的起始部分"研究现状"由背景信息、相关研究领域的现状、研究的价值和重要性、文献综述四个要素构成。每个要素在引言中发挥着不同的语篇功能，同时在写作范式上既有共性也有差异。

1. 背景信息

论文的性质、特点等因素决定了每一篇引言背景信息的独特性，背景信息的介绍在篇幅上不宜过长。此外，背景信息的写作一般以时间顺序展开，涉及对前人相关研究的梳理和回顾。因此，与时间概念相关的英文表达是学习重点，学习者有必要熟悉相关英文表达方式。以下列举部分时间表达方式，学习者可以根据具体的研究特点和个人习惯选择使用：

in recent years（近年来）

until quite recently（最近）

during the past decade（近10年来）

in the previous years（前几年）

in the successive years（连续几年来）

in the subsequent years（随后几年）

over the past three years（在过去的3年中）

in the early part of the century（本世纪初）

in the early spring of 1985（1985 年初春）

in the mid to late 1990s（20 世纪 90 年代中期到后期）

in the late 19th century（19 世纪末）

around 1990（1990 年前后）

since…（自从）

表示"早在年代/……中叶/……晚期"可选用

as early as the 1930s（早在 20 世纪 30 年代）

as far back as the 1980s（早在 20 世纪 80 年代）

as long ago as the 1960s（早在 20 世纪 60 年代）

in the early 1970s（在 20 世纪 70 年代初）

in the mid-twentieth century（在 20 世纪中叶）

during the late 20th century（在 20 世纪末叶）

参见下例：

例 1　**Over a period of several decades**, wavelet analysis has been applied to quite diverse fields.

近几十年来，……

例 2　Many of the suspension bridges built in the United States **in the 19th Century** are still in use today but…

在 19 世纪，……

例 3　**Since** the computer came into being, science and technology have made great advances.

自……以来，……

例 4　Remarkable developments can be seen in the field of optical fibre biosensors **in the last decade.**

在过去的十年间，……

例 5　Active vehicle suspension systems were introduced **in the early 1970s** to overcome the drawbacks of passive suspension.

20 世纪 70 年代初，……

2. 相关研究领域的现状

在引言写作的第一部分中，对相关研究领域现状的描述是一个不可或缺的要素。它是通过对当前研究相关领域发展过程的描述，说明该研究的历史性和延续性，从而说明当前研究领域的核心和热点研究地位，是进入当前研究核心的必要途径，起到承上启下的作用。同时，在这一部分的写作中，作者也可以提出自身的研究主题。该要素的写作范式、句式和措辞等见表 3-2。

表 3-2 相关研究领域现状的写作范式

主＋系＋表结构	…is/has been a subject of concern …is/has been a center of interest …is/has been a field of attention	……备受关注
There be 句型	There is an interest in… There has been an awareness in…	对于……呈现出关注
主＋谓＋（宾）结构	…received/has (have) received attention …generated/has (have) generated interest …deserve/deserves/deserved attention	……备受关注 ……引发关注 ……值得关注
被动语态	…is/are recognized as… （Attention）has been focused on… （Attention）is/has been put on… …is/has been diverted in/towards…	……被看作…… 对……一直予以关注 对……一直呈现出关注 关注重心转向……

参见下例：

例1 The safety of multistory reinforced-concrete buildings during construction **is a major concern.**

……问题是人们一直关注的主要问题。

例2 Infrastructure networks such as highways, pipelines, buildings, and water/sewer systems **have recently been at the center of attention for** contractors and owner organizations.

……问题近来备受关注。

例3 **The focus** of office computing today **has shifted from** automating individual work activities **to** supporting the automation of organization business processes.

对于……问题的研究重点从……向……转变。

例4 The effective use of computing in engineering **is recognized by many as the key to** increased individual, corporate, and national productivity.

……一直被认为是……的关键/核心。

引言第一部分中针对"相关研究领域的现状"的描述，亦可参见下列表述：

（1）… is/are a major concern.

……备受关注。

（2）… is a subject of much concern.

……是备受关注的课题。

（3）… is a subject of (considerable) current interest.

……是当前引起关注的课题。

（4）… is an active research field.

……是活跃的研究领域。

（5）The subject of … is of considerable current interest.

……课题近来引起广泛的研究兴趣。

（6）… have/has recently been at the center of attention.

……近来备受关注。

(7) In recent years, applied researchers have become increasingly interested in …

近年来,应用研究人员对……产生了越来越浓的兴趣。

(8) Of particular interest and complexity are …

……尤为引起关注。

(9) The relationship between … and … is a classic problem of …

……和……的关系一直是针对……的典型问题。

(10) The well-known phenomena … have been favorite topics for analysis in …

这些现象一直是进行……分析时最常探讨的话题。

(11) A central issue in … is …

……一直以来是……的核心问题。

(12) There has been a steady growth of interest in …

人们一直持续关注……

(13) There is current interest in …

人们近来关注……

(14) There has been increased awareness of the importance of …

对于……重要性的认识日益加深。

(15) Recently, there has been a spate of interest in how to …

近来人们对于如何……呈现出广泛的关注和兴趣。

(16) Recently, there has been wide interest in …

近来人们对于……有着广泛的关注和兴趣。

(17) There has been a growing concern about…

人们对……日益关注。

(18) The subject has received a great deal of recent attention…

……论题近来备受关注。

(19) A number of achievements in this field deserve special attention…

这一领域的众多成就值得特别关注/特别值得重视……

(20) The focus of … has shifted from … to …

对于……的研究重点已从……向……转变。

(21) The increasing interest in … has heightened the need for …

对于……的持续关注使得对……的研究成为必要。

(22) The possibility of … has generated interest in…

这一可能性引发了对于……的关注和兴趣。

(23) Many investigators have recently turned to…

近来,很多研究者将研究重心转向……

(24) As far back as…, attention was directed towards this problem.

早在……年代,人们就注意到了这一问题。

(25) …is recognized by many as the key to…

……被大家看作是……的关键。

(26) In recent years, considerable theoretical efforts have been put in …
近年来人们对……进行了大量理论研究。

(27) With the increasing interest in…, …
随着对……的关注,……

3. 研究的价值和重要性

从某种意义上讲,引言第一部分"研究现状"第二要素和第三个要素是一个整体,它们构成了相互映衬、相互补充的关系。在写作过程中,须根据该研究的性质和特点在描述上进行必要的细化,可以合二为一,也可以分开陈述。作为一个选择性要素,该要素是在描述相关研究领域现状的基础上,进一步揭示该研究的价值和重要性,同时对该研究核心的确立予以佐证。相关的常见词汇和表达(见表3-3)是学习的重点,同时应结合第二个要素的常见句型,进一步掌握该要素的写作特点。

表3-3 研究价值和重要性的写作范式

…is important…		……对于……很重要
…is significant…		……对于……很有意义
…is the key to…		……对于……很关键
The study of …has become an important aspect of…		……的研究对于……很重要
…play	an essential	role in…	……在……方面发挥着根本的作用
	an important		……在……方面发挥着重要的作用
	a vital		……在……方面发挥着至关重要的作用
	a primary		……在……方面发挥着主要的作用
	a fundamental		……在……方面发挥着基本的作用
	a crucial		……在……方面发挥着关键的作用
	a significant		……在……方面发挥着有意义的作用

参见下例:

例1 Sensitivity analysis is **an important method** for solving various optimization problems in transportation systems.
……是解决……的重要手段/方法/方式。

例2 Freight transport **plays an ever-increasing role in** the urban economy for several reasons.
……发挥着日益重要的作用。

例3 **It is, therefore, important to** model the behavior of confined concrete for noncircular sections.
……对于……很重要。

例4 This is **especially significant** in urban freight, where the benefits and impediments associated with high population densities are in direct conflict.
……尤其对……有重要意义。

例5 **The importance of** segmentation in the development of an effective marketing strategy **is well established** in the business literature.

……在……方面的重要性已经充分地得到了印证。

例 6　There has been **increased awareness of the importance of**…

人们对于……重要性的认识日益加深。

例 7　Preservation of these historic bridges **is important** since they are regarded as national treasures.

……一直很重要。

例 8　The effective use of computing in engineering is recognized by many **as the key to** increased individual, corporate, and national productivity.

……是……的关键。

4. 文献综述

"文献综述"是学术论文引言第一部分中的必需性要素,也是最后一个要素。文献综述中可以先对当前研究的相关内容进行概述和归纳,篇幅主要依据研究的特点和性质而定,可长可短,从而进一步凸显当前研究的必要性和重要性,为接下来详尽地回顾和总结前人的研究成果进行铺垫。需要注意的是,文献综述并非简单的罗列,因此,在这部分的写作中,须充分思考文献综述与当前研究的相关性。这一部分因研究不同而形式多样,应根据研究的具体情况而定,但大体可以归为两类:第一,对相关知识和操作的陈述;第二,对相关现象的陈述。

参见下例:

例 1　**Insight into** the behavior of pedestrians, and tools to predict this behavior, **are essential in** the planning and design of public pedestrian facilities such as airport, transfer stations, and shopping malls.

对于……深入了解是……的关键。

例 2　Induction motors **are widely used in industry because of** their reliability and relatively low cost.

由于……,……被广泛地用于……

例 3　Non-destructive evaluation (NDE) techniques, such as ultrasonic waves, eddy current, X-ray, infrared thermography, etc., **are extensively used in** the aerospace industry throughout the lifecycle of an aircraft.

……被广泛地运用于……

例 4　At the macro-scale, adhesion between contracting bodies **has a negligible effect** on surface interactions.

……对……的影响微不足道。

例 5　Cylindrical structures consisting of eccentric layers **are a common geometric form** in many fields, ranging from biological structures such as bones and blood vessels, to telecommunication infrastructure such as cables and optical fibres, to underground pipelines, and to many other mechanical and civil structures in almost all sizes.

……是很常见的几何图形。

在对当前研究的相关内容进行概述和归纳之后,须回顾和总结前人在相关领域的研究。然而,不同学科、不同性质的研究决定了这部分内容的个性化和多样性,但文献回顾内容之前的导入性话语发挥着承上启下的作用,在写作范式上具有很强的规律性,也是学习的重点。在时态上,根据相关研究的性质,可以使用一般现在时、一般过去时和现在完成时。此外,被动语态可以突出描述对象的性质、状态和结果,所以,除了主动语态,被动语态的使用也是这一要素写作范式中的一个重要话语特征。常用的表达范式有主动语态、被动语态和存在句型,如表3-4所示。

表3-4 文献综述的写作范式

主动语态	...has focused on... ...has concentrated on... ...has revealed... ...has demonstrated... ...has reported... ...has indicated...			……的研究集中于…… ……的研究专注于…… ……的研究说明…… ……的研究表明…… ……的研究提出…… ……的研究指出……
被动语态	Numerous Considerable Voluminous	efforts research studies tools techniques devices	have been achieved have been applied have been analyzed have been carried out have been conducted have been designed have been developed have been devoted have been researched have been put into have been presented have been proposed have been used have been utilized	大量的努力/研究/工具/技术/设计/手段 得以 进行/实现/使用/研发/研究/分析/投入/实施/提出/设计/运用
There be 句型	There is considerable/numerous/voluminous literature on ...			对于……,前人进行了大量的研究

参见下例:

1) 主动语态

例1 Workflow system **has gone through three stages** over the last decade.
……经历了三个发展阶段。

例2 **Considerable research effort has concentrated on** fuzzy logic, neural networks and artificial intelligence techniques.
大量的研究集中在……方面。

例3 **Early research focused primarily on** linear techniques, such as optimal control and skyhook control.
早期的研究主要集中在……方面。

例4 **An extensive literature review has revealed that** World Bank and its clients have developed their own consultant selection frameworks to improve the transparency of evaluation.

前人大量的研究表明……

例 5　**Early studies demonstrated** that the outcomes could be affected by the perceptual difference on the importance of the model.

早期的研究表明……

例 6　**A survey of literature indicated that** sliding mode control（SMC）is a highly effective nonlinear and robust control strategy.

前人的研究表明……

例 7　**Several writers have reported that** this irrigation system has the potential to conserve water as compared to level irrigation.

一些研究者曾提出……

例 8　**Efforts in** analyzing pattern recognition **have been relatively recent** compared with the long history of studies on offline signature verification.

对于……的研究才是近年的事。

2）被动语态

例 1　**A number of** simulation tools **have been developed** for this purpose, for example …

研发出很多……

例 2　In recent years, hardware-based value predictors **have been researched extensively** to predict the content of CPU registers.

近年，人们对……进行了大量的研究。

例 3　**A considerable amount of effort has been devoted to** designing a classifier particular to small sample size situations.

对于……投入了大量的精力。

例 4　**Numerous techniques like** surface modification **have been extensively analyzed and studied by researchers.**

研究人员对……进行了大量的分析和研究。

例 5　**Numerous studies have been conducted on** the adherence of spherical bodies.

人们在……方面进行了很多的研究。

例 6　**Considerable research has been carried out previously** for the development of various techniques for bearing fault detection and diagnosis based on vibration.

人们对……进行了大量的研究。

例 7　In the last two decades, many control algorithms and devices **have been proposed** for civil engineering applications.

人们对……提出了很多……

例 8　**A considerable amount of success has been achieved** in image indexing and retrieval techniques.

在……方面取得了重大成果。

例 9　Structural evaluations using dynamics-based methods **have become an increasingly utilized procedure for** nondestructive testing.

……越来越成为广泛使用的程序/方法。

例10　**This method has become widely used in** Japan, mainly due to track conditions.

这一方法广泛地应用于……

例11　In recent years, **considerable theoretical efforts have been put into** the new design of a falling film absorber.

近年来,人们对……进行了大量的理论研究。

例12　Over a period of several decades, wavelet analysis **has been set on a rigorous framework and has been applied to** quite a diverse field.

……已经形成了严格的框架并已应用于很多领域。

例13　Elegant synthetic routes to complicated covalent light-harvesting arrays **have been developed by several groups**, among which Lindsey's and Gossauer's achievements deserve special mention.

很多研究团队对……进行了研发。

例14　More about VLC **decoding methods have been designed** to deal with image or video stream with errors.

针对……,研究人员设计了很多方法。

例15　**The relationships between** vehicle mechanics and mobility **have been studied** by many authors.

很多研究者都对……和……的关系进行了研究。

3) There be 句型

例1　**There is voluminous body of literature focusing on** wavelet analysis.

前人对……进行了大量的研究。

例2　**There is no consensus among researchers regarding** the application of bi-modal network to optimal pricing.

对于……问题,学者的观点仍有分歧。

5. 范文分析

1) 范文一

S1: Sensitivity analysis **is an important method** for solving various optimization problems in transportation systems.　　研究领域的现状和价值

S2: Efficient computational algorithms for sensitivity analysis of the multinominal logit stochastic user equilibrium model **have been provided by** Clark and Watling which can deal with more general SUE models including the probit model.　　文献综述

(*Transportation Research*)

在这篇范文中,作者首先对研究领域的现状进行了描述,揭示了该研究的重要性,使描述有据可依,凸显该研究的学术价值和实用价值。在接下来的语句中,作者有选择性地重点回顾了两项前人研究,同时提供了更为具体的研究内容,充分呈现了文献综述与当前研究的相关性。

2) 范文二

S1-S2：Cylindrical structure consisting of eccentric layers **are a common geometric form in many fields**，ranging from biological structures such as bones and blood vessels，to telecommunication infrastructure such as cables and optical fibres，to underground pipelines，and to many other mechanical and civil structures in almost all sizes. Efforts in analyzing wave scattering characteristics by such structures have been relatively recent，compared to the long history of studies on sound and wave propagation.

相关研究领域的现状

S3-S9：In 1974，Shaw and Tai first formulated the acoustic scattering by a two-layer eccentric cylinder using the boundary integral method. It was later extended to elastic longitudinal and shear wave problems. The normal mode expansion method was used for electromagnetic waves and the diffusion of neutrons in a nuclear reactor. By that time，approximate results were obtained by using a perturbation method for small eccentricities. The perturbation method remains a useful method for approximate solutions. More recently，exact numerical results have been obtained. In addition，Danila et al. used a generalized Debye series expansion to describe the physical process by reflection and transmission coefficients for each normal mode. Kishk et al. formulated the problem of scattering of electromagnetic waves by a scatterer of an arbitrary number of layers. Ioannidou et al. formulated the problem of scattering of electromagnetic waves by multiple scatterers enclosed within a cylindrical enclosure and by multiple eccentric multilayer scatterers enclosed by an eccentrically stratified cylinder.

文献综述

(QJMAM [*The Quarterly Journal of Mechanics & Applied Mathematics*])

在这篇范文中，作者先引出相关研究话题，说明当前研究一直为众多研究者所关注，接下来又通过一个拓展句进行了进一步概述，而这篇范文主体则是 S3-S9，以时间为线索对前人在这一领域的研究进行了系统、全面的回顾和总结，篇幅较长。

"研究现状"是引言的第一部分，其中有三个要素是必须涵盖的要素。中国研究者在引言写作中不同程度地存在一些问题，如引述前人研究成果时，信息来源标注不清，标注方式不规范等,文献综述的内容往往不够翔实和系统。这在一定程度上说明作者缺乏对前人研究的系统回顾和总结,篇幅通常较短,不仅不能达到写作目的,而且无法发挥承上启下的作用。更重要的是,文献综述不够全面、系统,一定程度上无法充分体现当前研究的价值所在,因而影响学术交流的质量和效果。

3.3.2 研究中心的写作范式

"研究中心"是学术论文引言的中间环节,作者可以指出前人研究的不足,提出需要解决的问题,也可以在前人研究基础上接续研究。在这一部分的写作中,作者须根据自身研究的特点和性质选择其中任何一个要素作为具体的实现手段。"前人研究的不足"这一要素是引言写作第二部分中使用频度最高的步骤。作者通过指出前人研究的不足,不仅可以表明作者对前人相关研究有充分而系统的掌握和了解,同时可以揭示当前研究的核心内容,从而突出该研究的创新点,并进一步烘托研究的意义、价值、重要性、学术性或实用性等。由于这一要素普遍为作者采用,因此该要素的写作范式是学习的重点。

1. 前人研究的不足

"前人研究的不足"是学术论文引言写作第二部分中最常使用的步骤,常通过转折关系的表达和句式(见表3-5)指出前人研究具体的不足,进而引出当前研究的中心。

表3-5 前人研究不足的写作范式

转折关系	Despite... However, ... Although ...	尽管…… 然而,…… 尽管……
否定词汇及表达的使用	ignore, need, necessary, drawback, limitation, limit, gap, problem, little, few, not ... suitable, not ... practical, not ... feasible	忽视,需要,有必要,缺点,限制,局限,差距,问题,很少,不适合,不实用,不可行

参见下例:

1) 表示转折关系的介词短语

例1 **Despite** the recent recognition of the contribution of freight transportation to the performance of urban areas under the rubric of city logistics, **we see a void in** the study of how the stakeholders in the supply chain might cooperate through participation in distribution networks, to reduce the costs associated with traffic congestion.

尽管……,但在……方面的研究依旧是空白。

例2 **Despite** their published benefits, these systems remain complex, bulky, and expensive and are not common options on production vehicles.

尽管……,这些系统依旧……

2) 表示转折关系的副词

例1 **This, however, represents a major challenge** since maintenance operation for infrastructure networks are usually carried out under stringent resource and tie constraints.

然而,这对……构成重要挑战。

例 2　**However**, these approaches are **either** complex in their theoretical bases **or** difficult to practically implement.

然而,这些方法要么……要么……

例 3　Early research focused primarily on linear techniques, such as optimal control and skyhook control. **However**, vehicle suspensions contain dynamic nonlinearities associated with springs and dampers, sliding friction in joints and nonlinear kinematics which **significantly affect** ride quality and handling performance.

早期研究集中于……,但……对……有很大影响。

例 4　**However**, a geometrically linear theory **is not well adapted to the design** of suspension bridges with long spans, shallow trusses, or a large dead load.

然而,……理论并不完全适用于……

例 5　**However**, **few** conservation scientists or conservationists **seem to be aware of** the implications of the directions that have emerged regarding PA (Protected Area) classification or the new paradigm.

然而,科研工作者对……认识不够。

例 6　**However**, diagnosis and isolation of both electrical and mechanical faults of an induction motor **is a challenging problem.**

然而,……是一个具有挑战性的问题。

例 7　**However, it is impractical**, both financially and logistically, for all researchers in structural control to conduct even small-scale experimental tests.

但是,……是不切实际的。

例 8　Existing techniques for delay analysis, **however**, having been developed and used to settle delay claims after project completion, **may not be totally suitable for** schedule compression since delay liabilities need to be determined during the progress of the project.

然而,……未必完全适用于……

3) 让步状语从句

例 1　**Although** the retrieval is very fast, **this index does not** provide a high retrieval rate.

尽管……,这一指数并未……

例 2　**Although** this technique has good indexing performance, the computational complexity is very high.

尽管……,……

例 3　**Although** there are more and more successes in the workflow research and development, **it is widely recognized that there are still technical problems**, ranging from inflexible and rigid process specification and execution mechanisms.

尽管……,在……方面还存在公认的技术问题。

例 4　**Although** there is a growing and informative literature on alternative frameworks for designing freight distribution networks in a supply chain, **there appears to**

be a void in taking the recognized set of alternative distribution networks and formally establishing how agents in a supply chain might cooperate.

尽管……，在……方面还存在空白。

例 5　**Although** there has been much interest in the design of the suspended model, **there have been few studies** of the applications of it.

尽管……，但是对于……的研究尚不多见。

4）具有否定含义的词汇及表达

除了使用以上表示转折关系的句式外，可以通过使用具体词汇以及具有否定意义的表达说明当前研究的不足和局限。

例 1　**The primary drawbacks of such methods** include the ad hoc nature of controller synthesis and absence of robustness guarantees.

这些方法最主要的缺陷是……

例 2　**Not many investigations** on these effects can be found in the literature.

以往对于……的研究尚不多见。

例 3　Almost all commercial project management software systems, for example, are based on the critical path method and, as such, **exhibit some serious drawbacks.**

……呈现出严重不足。

例 4　Traditional fractal parameters **have some inherent drawbacks.**

……有内在的缺陷。

例 5　**There are two potential limitations** with existing decomposition methods.

……存在两个潜在局限。

例 6　There are several important issues **that have not been adequately addressed.**

对……的探讨还不够完善。

例 7　Consequently, **there is a need for** conceptually different strategies, algorithms, and tools in hardware design.

对……有必要进行……

例 8　**Relatively few papers are devoted to the studies of** solvent extraction of the rare earth ions with PAN.

对于……的研究还远远不够。

例 9　**Little is known about** the biotic and abiotic characteristics of effluents from shrimp facilities as well as the environmental load.

对于……研究甚少。

例 10　**Previous researchers have ignored** the requirements that economic theory places on optimizing behavior for any area to have a common currency.

前人的研究忽略了……

例 11　**Not many investigations** on the application of the new technique can be found in the literature.

研究人员未对……作充分的调查研究。

引言中"前人研究的不足"这一要素亦可参见下列表述：

(1) To eliminate these drawbacks, we have developed...

为了消除这些不足,我们研发了……

(2) A more exact theory is required to...

需要一个更精确的理论来……

(3) ...is not yet practicable.

……还不具实用性。

(4) It is not yet feasible to...

……还不可行。

(5) The problem is that ...

问题在于……

(6) To our knowledge, little attention has been given to ...

对……关注还远远不够。

(7) Although there are more and more successes in..., it is widely recognized that there are still technical problems.

尽管……,但是……

(8) Few scientists seem to be aware of ...

很少有研究者认识到……

(9) Consequently, there is a need for ...

有必要进行……

(10) ...has/have some inherent drawbacks...

……存在内在的缺点。

(11) Existing techniques for...may not be totally suitable for...

……对于……并不完全适合。

(12) ...exhibit some serious drawbacks.

……呈现出严重不足。

(13) Relatively few papers are devoted to the studies of...

对于……的研究还相对较少。

(14) There are no published data for...

对于……尚无公开数据。

(15) Owing to/due to the lack of...

由于缺乏……

(16) This is at the expense of some loss in..., although accuracies in... have been reported in the literature.

尽管……,却是以……为代价的。

(17) More integrated approach is needed to complement existing approaches.

尚需更完整的方法来……

(18) Not many investigations on...can be found in the literature.

在……方面进行的调查还不充分。

(19) In marked contrast to the extensive studies of…, very few studies of…have been reported.

对于……的研究还非常有限。

(20) Ongoing research set out in the paper is designed to contribute to filling this void.

当前研究意在弥补……的不足。

(21) No studies on…are available…

尚无对……方面的研究。

除了要素1(指出前人研究的不足)，引言写作的第二部分还有以下要素可供选择：要素2(提出需要解决的问题)、要素3(继续前人的研究)。由于要素2和要素3不太为研究者采用，在引言写作中并不多见，此处不做详述。

参见下例：

例1 **Our research extends the concept** of "aspect" to encompass orthogonal end-user visible requirements of the system.

当前研究拓展了……的概念。

例2 **A more integrated approach is needed to complement** existing approaches.

需要一个更综合的方法对……进行补充。

例3 **The problem presented herein is an extension of** the seismically excited next generation benchmark problem presented at the Second World Conference on Structural Control to include nonlinear responses and to address other building heights.

当前的议题是对……的拓展。

例4 It is **in this broader meaning of the concept of** scenarios that we propose a framework for applying scenario planning to regional strategic transportation planning.

在更为宽泛的概念背景下，……

2. 范文分析

1) 范文一

…**However**, the between-class scatter matrix as selection criterion used by these approaches cannot be computed due to the special characteristics of signature verification that training samples come from genuine class only. Hence, these approaches **are not applicable** in the study to estimate stable class statistics.

前人研究的不足

(*IEEE Transactions on Systems, Man, and Cybernetics*)

在这篇范文中，作者通过指出前人研究的不足来确立论文的研究中心。作者先使用了表示转折关系的副词结构，进而使用了具体词汇"applicable"的否定形式指出以往研究模式的缺陷，从而确立了当前研究的重心。

2) 范文二

The problem is that traces from interesting applications tend to be very large. For example, collecting just one byte of information per executed instruction generates on the order of a gigabyte of data per second of CUP time on a high-end microprocessor. **Moreover**, traces from many different programs are typically collected to capture a wide variety of workloads. Storing the resulting multigigabyte traces can be a challenge, even on today's large head disks.

前人研究的不足

（*IEEE Transactions on Computers*）

在这篇范文中，作者首先通过简洁的句式结构（The problem is that...）对前人的研究提出疑问，然后通过"moreover"句式进一步清晰地指出了前人研究存在的局限，从而确定了当前的研究中心。

3) 范文三

Bunch and Griffin studied colloidal particle removal in the contract stabilization activated sludge process, and concluded that removal of colloidal substrate was essentially complete in 5 min regardless of the amount of colloidal material initially present. **However**, these authors calculated the colloidal concentrations at time zero from mass balance considerations rather than measuring them, and this, in most cases, led to reporting negative colloidal concentration at times greater than zero.

前人研究的不足

（*Journal of Environmental Engineering*）

在这篇范文中，作者在对前人研究进行回顾总结之后，通过使用表示转折关系的副词结构，指出前人研究的不足，从而确定了该论文的研究中心。

3.3.3　研究目的与意义的写作范式

学术论文引言的第三部分是对前文提到的不足予以解答，主要陈述当前研究的目的和意义，此外，亦可对主要结果进行概括性描述。该部分由研究目的、研究内容、研究结果、用途启示及后续研究和结构框架五个要素构成。

1. 研究目的

"研究目的"是引言第三部分中的一个必需性要素，主要描述研究的目的，句意功能单纯，有很强的规律性，并非学习难点，掌握该要素在词汇和句式上的突出特征是学习的重点。研究目的写作范式如表3-6所示。

表 3-6　研究目的的写作范式

The aim of the work is to… The focus of the study is to… The target of the essay is to… The purpose of the paper is to… The goal of the research is to… The scope of the thesis is to… The target of the article is to… The objective of the project is to…	本研究的目的是……
The paper aims to… The work aims at… The design targets at… The essay attempts to… The study sets out to… The project is aimed at… The thesis is targeted at…	本研究旨在……

参见下例：

例1　**The purpose of this work is to** document the performance of bonded bridge deck overlays that have been placed in Alabama.

本研究的目的是……

例2　The algorithms presented in this paper **aim at** minimizing these downsides.

本文旨在……

例3　**The aim of this research was to** assess the influence of environmental factors and management practices on these water quality variables as well as to identify the most important relationships established among these key variables.

本研究的目的是……

例4　**The purpose of this paper is to** examine the new paradigm, its relationship to the IUCN (The World Conservation Union) PA (protected Areas) category system and its implications for protected areas and wild biodiversity.

本文的目的是……

例5　**The main objective of this paper is to** quantify the effect of human error and error control measures in multistory RC (reinforced-concrete) building failures during construction.

本文的主要目的是……

例6　In this paper, we **concentrate our discussion on** the problem of flexibility and extensibility of process specification and execution mechanisms.

本文将主要讨论……

例7　**The purpose of this work is to** develop effective sensitivity analysis methods for solving various optimization problems in a combined transport system.

这项工作的目的是……

例8　**This paper sets out to** define a new set of problems which occurs in the context of mobile communication.

本文将着手对……

引言第三部分中针对"研究目的"的表达，亦可参见下列表述：

（1）This paper has three primary purposes...

本文主要有三个目的……

（2）The goal of the present study is to...

当前研究的目的是……

（3）The main objective of the present paper is to...

本文研究的主要目的是……

（4）The aim of this work is to...

本研究的目标是……

（5）The paper aims to...

本文旨在……

（6）The study targets/aims at...

本研究意在……

（7）The present research attempts to...

本研究试图……

（8）The present effort is an attempt to...

当前研究意在……

（9）The focus point of this paper is...

本文的核心要点是……

（10）To achieve the goal, ...

为了实现这个目标，……

（11）In order to bring this problem to a clear understanding...

为了澄清这个问题，……

（12）This paper sets out to...

这篇论文针对……

（13）The scope of this study on... is composed of several tasks...

本研究涉及几项任务……

（14）The motivation behind the present study is to establish a relationship between... and...

本研究的动机意在……

（15）The purpose of this study is twofold：first... second...

本研究有两重研究目的，一是……，二是……

2. 研究内容

"研究内容"是引言第三部分中的又一个必需性步骤，在说明研究目的之后，作者须针对研究内容的相关信息，如研究的特点、性质、方法、价值、重要性、意义等，有选择地进行补充，因此有时可以将要素1（研究目的）和要素2（研究内容）合二为一。研究内容的写作范式如

表 3-7 所示。

表 3-7 研究内容的写作范式

主动语态	The paper investigates…	本文调查了……
	The work presents…	本研究呈现了……
	The analysis examines…	这项分析检测了……
	The approach uses…	这一方法使用了……
	The method employs…	这一方法运用了……
	The study describes…	本研究描述了……
	The research utilizes…	本研究运用了……
	The project demonstrates…	这一项目呈现了……
被动语态	…is/was performed	本文对……进行了实施
	…is/was carried out	本文对……进行了调查
	…is/was investigated	本文对……进行了调查
	…is/was examined	本文对……进行了检测
	…is/was established	本文确定……
	…is/was proved	本文证实了……

参见下例：

1) 主动语态

例1 **This paper employed a framework to investigate** how agents in a retail supply chain might interact more effectively to reduce the costs of urban freight distribution.

本文运用了一个框架体系对……进行了调查。

例2 **This paper investigates** the application of robust, nonlinear observation and control strategies, namely sliding mode observation and control, to semiactive vehicle suspensions using a model reference approach.

本文调查了……

例3 **The approach presented here employs and improves** the design of the traditional control and **advances** the previous control.

本文提出的方法使用、改进了……，并发展了……

例4 **This paper presents** the formulation of a new distributed scheduling model that facilitates the planning and scheduling of resources in large networks with repetitive nontypical tasks and spatially distributed sites.

本文呈现了……

例5 **Such a framework is a powerful way of investigating** the behavioral response of each agent to many policies, including congestion pricing, as a way of improving the efficient flow of traffic in cities.

这样的框架对于调查……非常有效。

例6 **This modification improves the performance of** the FC technique by reducing the dissimilarity between the fractal codes of the query image and candidate images.

这一改进提高了……的性能。

例7 Elastic-plastic-creep **analysis is performed to study** the behavior of beam structures under load and deformation-controlled conditions.

本文运用……分析来研究……

例 8　**This paper examines** the suitability of current delay analysis techniques.

本文检测了……

例 9　**The present study uses** a probability-based safety analysis to assess the effect of construction error on the performance of multistory RC（reinforced-concrete）buildings during construction.

本研究使用了……

例 10　**This article describes** new and important experimental findings of pedestrian flow theory, in particular, pertaining to behavior of pedestrians and characteristics of pedestrian flows in the case of bottlenecks.

本文描述了……

例 11　**This paper presents a quantitative description of** the dynamics of water quality variables monitored in influents and effluents.

本文呈现了对于……的量化分析。

例 12　**This account summarizes** some of our efforts in equipping synthetic chromophores with groups that under appropriate conditions induce self-assembly.

这一报告总结了……

例 13　**The design utilizes** the unused vertical spacing between the coolant tubes to form the falling film.

该设计使用了……

2）被动语态

例 1　**In this paper**, cyclic loading analysis of beams under different types of loading such as thermal, mechanical and their combinations **is investigated.**

本文就……，进行了调查。

例 2　**A static analysis is carried out to** achieve the deformed equilibrium configuration.

为了……，进行了静态分析。

例 3　**A model analysis is performed to** determine the significant material and structural parameters.

通过模型分析来……

例 4　**A simple model was established to** predict the behavior of the detector.

建立了简单的模型用于……

3. 研究结果

"研究结果"是引言第三部分的一个选择性步骤，该要素应简单扼要地描述主要的研究结果和发现，根据具体的研究性质和特点，还可以对研究结果进行必要的佐证。需要注意的是，一篇学术论文有独立的部分对研究结果进行详尽、系统的陈述，所以引言部分针对研究成果的描述篇幅不宜过长。该部分常用的词汇有 accomplish, confirm, exhibit, prove, reveal, show, turn out, utilize, validate, verify, yield 等，常用写作范式如表 3-8 所示。

表 3-8　研究结果的写作范式

主动语态	The results showed…	结果显示了……
	The experiment revealed…	实验显示了……
	The technique exhibited…	技术显示了……
	The system validated…	系统证实了……
	The analysis proved…	分析证实了……
	The design established…	设计证实了……
	The approach verified…	方法证实了……
	The assessment confirmed…	评测证实了……
	The test justified…	试验证明了……
	The results accomplished…	结果实现了……
	The model analysis demonstrated…	模型分析显示了……
	It turned out that…	结果显示……
	We yielded the following results…	我们得出以下结果……
被动语态	It is/has been shown that…	
	It is/has been found that…	结果显示……
	It is/has been revealed that…	

参见下例：

例 1　**The results of these simulations reveal** the benefits of sliding mode observation and control for improved ride quality, and should be directly transferable to commercial semiactive vehicle suspension implementations.

模拟仿真的研究结果显示……

例 2　**It has been shown that** the solution procedure is analytically exact, and is suitable for all types of waves.

结果显示……

例 3　**It turns out that** the real area of contact is approximately proportional to the normal force.

结果表明……

例 4　**The result is consistent with** the adhesion theory of friction.

结果与……一致/吻合。

例 5　**We yielded the following results**…

我们得出以下结果……

例 6　**The results are verified against** the known experimental and analytical data given in the literature.

本研究结果与……截然相反。

例 7　**The experiments also confirmed** that a very high absorption heat duty could be accomplished in a compact absorber.

实验证实了……

例 8　**The technique shows** promising improvements in heat exchanger technology.

这一技术显示了……

例 9　The merit of existing methods should not be overlooked, **and indeed both the current and proposed methods are complementary.**

……,事实上现有的以及新提出的方法能够互相补充。

4. 用途启示及后续研究

"用途启示及后续研究"是引言第三部分的另一个选择性步骤。该要素在写作模式上相对灵活,在说明主要发现和结果之后,作者可以根据研究的特点和性质,指出该研究的局限以及今后的研究方向,从而在一定程度上体现出作者谦虚严谨的治学态度;亦可针对研究的应用情况和应用前景进行简要说明。

参见下例:

例 1　**The model will serve as the baseline for** the structural evaluation of the bridge. The baseline structural evaluations provide important design information that will assist in the preservation of the Roebling suspension bridge, and **furthermore**, the methodology developed in the research **can be applied to** a wider range of historic cable-supported bridges.

这一模式可以作为……的基准。此外,本研究的方法亦可应用于……

例 2　**This analysis will help in** comparing the proposed design with the current state-of-the-art absorber design.

这一分析结果对……很有帮助。

例 3　**Future work should include the analysis of** the transition from sliding to rolling and applications to technological problems. **It should also address** the analysis of the three-dimensional problem for sliding and rolling motions.

今后应该进一步对……进行分析研究。同时,应该对……进行分析。

例 4　**This concept may have application in** work on route guidance, as well as in emergency response, contingency planning, and transportation planning.

这一概念可运用于……

例 5　**The results** presented here **have implications for** long-term water policy, planning, and management in California.

研究结果对……有一定的启示。

例 6　**Although** our work is far from complete, **it does provide a general methodological framework for** the future study.

尽管……,但对于……提供了大体的方法框架。

例 7　**The system has the following advantages over** the existing ground-coil-based location system. (1) If the system loses its present location, this system can be restored in a second. The coil-based system cannot be restored until the next reference point. (2) In the case of the coil-based system, it is necessary that the onboard system can recognize the ground coil number to find the position information of ground coil.

这一系统有以下优点……

引言第三部分针对"用途启示和后续研究"的表达可参见下列表述:

(1) It can shed new light on the issues regarding...

……为……指明了方向。

(2) It may have application in work on...

……在……方面有应用价值。

(3) The measure may prove useful in…
这一措施可以在……的规划方面发挥有益作用。

(4) This is a preliminary attempt to analyze…
这是针对……的分析的一项初步尝试。

(5) Our research is applicable to…
我们的研究可以运用于……

(6) The results will be extended to other areas…
研究结果可以延伸到其他领域……

(7) The framework presented here can be extended to…
当前的框架可以推广到……

(8) These issues will be addressed in future studies of…
这些问题将在日后的……研究中予以讨论和解决。

(9) This study represents a first step towards…
本研究是对于……的初步研究。

(10) It is expected that … will continue to play a role in…
我们期望……将在……方面继续发挥作用。

(11) Further work needs to be done in…
在……方面还须进行进一步的研究。

(12) The present research aims to provide a basis for…
本文为……提供研究基础。

(13) The model will serve as a reference point for…
这一模型对……具有参考价值。

(14) The methodology developed under the framework can be applied to…
……可以运用于……

5．结构框架

"结构框架"是引言第三部分的又一个选择性要素，该要素描述论文的结构框架和内容安排，在英文学术论文中非常多见。中外学术论文撰写者对于这一要素有不同的写作习惯，作者可自己确定篇幅长度，为读者在后文的阅读中呈现出清晰的脉络，但是国内学者较少使用这一要素，这在一定程度上是中文学术论文的写作习惯带来的负面影响。因此，尽管"结构框架"是一个选择性步骤，论文初学者应充分重视这一要素的特点和功能，以免造成学术交流中不必要的障碍。引言结构框架写作范式如表3-9所示。

表3-9　结构框架的写作范式

主动语态	The research outlines…	本研究概述了……
	The report provides …	本研究报告提供了……
	The analysis discusses…	本文讨论了……
	The paper presents…	本文呈现了……
	The section estimates…	这一部分评估了……
	The method section analyzes…	方法部分分析了……
	The rest of the paper proceeds as follows…	论文其他部分组织如下……
	The organization of the paper is as follows…	论文的组织如下……

续表

被动语态	...is/are discussed in... ...is/are analyzed in... ...is/are presented in... ...is/are estimated in... The rest of the paper is organized as follows... The remainder of the paper is organized as follows...	……部分讨论了…… ……部分分析了…… ……部分呈现了…… ……部分评估了…… 论文剩余部分组织如下…… 论文剩余部分组织如下……

此外,由于这一要素的语篇功能较为单纯,在词汇使用上亦有规律可循。以下为部分高频词汇:advance, analyze, apply, attempt, close with, compute, conclude, confirm, consist of, describe, deserve, design, develop, development, discuss, document, effective, employ, enable, establish, estimate, evaluate, explain, feasible, finally, focus on, formulate, illustrate, improve, introduce, intend, investigate, methodology, obtain, offer, open with, organize, outline, overview, perform, practical, predict, present, prove, provide, report, summarize, ultimate, utilize, etc.

6. 范文分析

1)范文一

S1:This paper **presents a quantitative description of** the dynamics of water quality variables monitored in influents and effluents during two consecutive growout cycles at four shrimp acquaculture farms (two semi-intensive and two intensive acquaculture systems) located in the State of Sinaloa, Mexico. 研究内容

S2:**The aim of this research was to assess** the influence of environmental factors and management practices on these water quality variables **as well as to identify** the most important relationships established among these key variables. 研究目的

(*Water Environment Research*)

这篇范文由两个长句构成。第一句描述了该研究的主要内容,说明了该研究的特点和性质,烘托出了该研究的价值和意义;第二句陈述了研究目的。从范文可以看出,该研究有两个目的,作者通过使用"as well as"结构指出了研究的双重目的。

2)范文二

S1:**The aim of this paper is to devise** a more objective framework for general capabilities evaluation (GCE) so as to avoid any discrepancies in consultant pre-selection decisions. 研究目的

S2-S4：The paper **begins by** summarizing the commonly used criteria for GCE. The importance of CPC **is discussed**, and any perceptual differences between the client and consultant groups **are examined**. **Finally**, a multi-criteria model for consultant pre-selection **is proposed**.　　结构框架

(*Engineering, Construction and Architectural Management*)

　　这篇范文由两部分构成。第一部分通过一个长句说明了研究目的；第二部分由三个句子构成，详细说明了论文其他部分的结构框架和内容安排。

3) 范文三

This paper has three primary purposes. First, by situating scenario planning within the broader regional transportation-planning process and its relevant tools, the paper attempts to show the reader where and how scenario planning might make a contribution. **Second**, by documenting the methodology as applied to the Houston case, the paper intends to offer a specific step-by-step framework which practitioners might use in combination with their traditional regional transportation-planning process. The framework offers a structured, logical process—to enable consistency and deeper understanding—for depicting how the future we are planning for might evolve. **Finally**, by evaluating the approach used in the Houston case, the paper attempts to offer insights from the process, discussing links to other existing methodologies and suggesting extensions to the work. The ultimate goal of this work is to advance the development of an effective framework for improving strategic regional transportation planning in a world of uncertainty.　　研究目的

(*Journal of Urban Planning and Development*)

　　这篇范文由多个分句构成，整体结构以陈述研究目的为主线，开门见山，用一个单句简洁明了地说明本研究共有三个研究目的，使用了逻辑衔接语 first，second，finally；在研究目的的叙述中，贯穿了该研究的特点、性质以及方法等信息，内容翔实，是一个将研究目的和研究特性相结合进行描述的典型例子。

3.3.4 引言全文范文分析

　　本节摘选出五篇英文学术论文的引言全文，这五篇引言全文篇幅较为短小。通过分析范文，可以清晰地看到学术论文引言的结构特征和语言特征。其中，范文一、范文二和范文三的构成要素按照常见顺序进行排列，而范文四和范文五则出现了构成要素的内嵌和颠倒现象。因研究特点和性质的不同，写作要素的颠倒、交叉、复现、轮替现象在学术论文引言的写作中非常多见，因此熟悉引言的结构要素对于正确、有效地解读、撰写引言至关重要。

1. 范文一

引言第一部分：

The importance of segmentation in the development of an effective marketing strategy is **well established** in the business literature.

There are many bases used for market segmentation, but demographic factors such as age, occupation, income level, educational attainment, and race are frequently used to identify key markets. **Race has become increasingly important** as a segmentation variable because it has been shown that race can influence consumption patterns and because racial minorities have come to represent a larger and larger proportion of the U. S. population. The sheer numbers of the largest minority group, African-Americans, and the improving economic status of many of its members, make this racial minority especially attractive.

研究的价值和重要性

研究领域的现状

引言第二部分：

Nevertheless, relatively few studies in the finance literature have profiled differences in financial asset portfolio holdings of Black versus White households, or examined how these differences should affect the manner in which financial planners tailor their marketing efforts to meet the needs of different racial group.

前人研究的不足

引言第三部分：

The purpose of this study is twofold: First, we seek to profile racial differences in investment asset ownership patterns between Black and White households, evaluating the extent to which this profile is consistent with information reported in other academic work that examines racial differences in wealth accumulation patterns and risk tolerance levels. **Second,** we seek to use the profile of financial asset portfolio holdings reported here to advise financial planners and others in the financial community how to structure their product offerings to more effectively meet the needs of African-American consumers.

The balance of this study provides information and insights regarding the financial holdings and investment asset consumption preferences of Black and White households. **Section Ⅰ profiles** the growth of African-American households in recent years and surveys

研究目的

the literature to ascertain extant knowledge about differences in Black versus White financial asset portfolio holdings. **Section Ⅱ introduces** the SCF dataset that represents the source of the statistical information reported in the article, and explains the statistical tests used to compare Black versus White households. **Section Ⅲ presents** some of the principal differences in asset holding patterns across Black and White consumers, controlling for income, age, and educational attainment in presenting household financial information across different racial groups. **Section Ⅳ uses** the information introduced in Section Ⅲ to develop a profile of African-American households' wealth-building asset portfolios for financial planners seeking to understand and serve the needs of the African-American market segment. **Finally, Section Ⅴ provides** conclusions regarding the differences between Black and White financial consumers and summarizes how these differences influence asset holdings patterns across the two racial groups.

结构框架

(*Financial Services Review*)

2. 范文二

引言第一部分：

Water is scarce in California. Significant spatial and temporal variability of water supplies has led to construction of a vast intertied network of reservoirs, aqueducts, wells, and recharge and reuse facilities throughout the state. Competition between agricultural, urban, and environmental demands has intensified with population growth and increasing environmental allocations.

研究背景

引言第二部分：

The complexity of selecting efficient water management alternatives at both state and regional levels suggests that perhaps **a different, more integrated approach is needed** to complement existing simulation-based planning approaches.

继续前人的研究

引言第三部分：

This paper outlines results from a study utilizing CALVIN, a model combining ideas from economics and engineering optimization with advances in software and data to suggest more integrated management of water supplies regionally and throughout California.

研究内容

The results presented here **have implications for** long-term water policy, planning, and management in California.   研究应用前景

(Journal of Water Resources Planning and Management)

3. 范文三
引言第一部分：

Tilting trains in Japan have an onboard database to store the position, curvature, cant and other curve dimensional information, to control the body tilt angle and to cancel the unbalanced centrifugal acceleration calculated from curve dimensions and running speed. This control system works predicatively to prevent service disruption caused by controlled delays at tight curves, which are commonplace on narrow gauge lines in Japan. It is essential for these types of tilting trains to accurately detect their running position. For this purpose, it is normally the case that trains calculate the running distance by monitoring the number of wheel revolutions and using the ground coils installed on the track for the automatic train stop system as position reference points. This control method has become widely used in Japan, mainly due to track conditions. Another reason is that, to raise the curve negotiating speed without increasing the body roll angular velocity on narrow gauge lines in Japan, where sharp curves with short transition curves predominate, it is advantageous to predict the required body tilt angle before entering a curve and to control the body tilt accordingly thereafter on the curve.   研究领域的现状

引言第二部分：

However, this method requires the onboard database to be updated continuously, which places great demands on manpower. In addition, position reference points may be lost when wheels slip.   前人研究的不足

引言第三部分：

To eliminate these drawbacks, we have developed a new train position detection system using GPS, which can automatically create a track database. In the field of railway vehicles, a number of applications, such as traffic management and control, have being considered. These applications do not require such exact position information compared with the tilting control application.   研究内容

This system has the following advantages over the existing ground-coil-based location system. (1) If the system loses its present location, this system can be restored in a second. The coil-based system cannot be restored until the next reference point. (2) In the case of the coil-based system, it is necessary that the onboard system can recognize the ground coil number to find the position information of ground coils. For this purpose, the coil system needs very expensive devices, such as the transponder units. GPS provides absolute location by using only a low-cost onboard system. Therefore, this system ensures higher stability and greater precision in position detection than the existing system.　　用途启示

This report outlines the new system and describes precision-verifying test results.　　研究内容

(*Quarterly of Report of RTRI*)

4. 范文四
引言第一部分和第二部分：

Performance of circular concrete columns subjected to axial compressive loads improves dramatically with fiber-reinforced polymer composite (FRP) wraps on them. FRP wrapping is not as effective for columns of noncircular cross section or when the load is applied eccentrically. In civil construction, the majority of columns are either square or rectangular in cross section. The analytical model for a standard circular column under the axisymmetric condition is not applicable for noncircular sections.　　研究领域的现状

It is, therefore, important to model the behavior of confined concrete for noncircular sections. In practice, columns have much higher slenderness ration than the standard specimens used in experiments. They are also subjected to eccentric loading.　　研究的价值和重要性

A model that includes all these effects becomes too complicated for design purposes. **An alternative is to** modify the axisymmetric short column models to include these effects. **Not many investigations on these effects can be found in the literature.** Mirmiran et al. proposed a minimum corner radius for the noncircular column wraps to be effective. Rochette and Labossiere proposed a ratio of corner radius over the width of column for rectangular and square column. Suter and Pinzelli studies the effect of the corner radius and concluded that a 5 mm corner radius was too small and a 25 mm radius was　　前人研究的不足和文献综述

adequate. Vintzileou demonstrated a model based on the statistical study of experimental and analytical works on prismatic column due to stress concentrations at the corners. Manfredi and Realfonzo used the iterative method of Spoelstra and Monti to consider the passive nature of confinement. A study on slender circular column was also reported .

引言第三部分：

The motivation behind the present study is to establish a relationship between these complicated effects and the model based on perfectly axisymmetric assumptions.   研究目的

We study the complicating effects cross-sectional shape and geometric as well as loading imperfections on the mechanical behavior of FRP-wrapped columns. Experiments have been conducted to record the complicating effects. The axisymmetric model has been modified to incorporate those effects. The proposed model has been validated with the present as well as previously reported experimental results.   研究内容

（Journal of Composites for Construction）

5. 范文五

引言第一部分和第二部分：

The range of potential environmental effects of the aquaculture activities depends on the type of culture developed: the managerial practices; and the physical, chemical, and biological characteristics of the location in which cultivation takes place.   研究领域的现状

Considering that **little is known about** the biotic and abiotic characteristics of effluents from shrimp farming in subtropical latitudes, the data provided in this paper can be useful in developing management strategies that allow production optimization, minimize the conflict of water use among productive activities, and reduce the environmental effects of shrimp farming activities.   前人研究的不足

Although the shrimp aquaculture development rate in Mexico has been relatively moderate, as in other countries it has brought concern about the possible effects of aquaculture pond effluents on the surrounding coastal ecosystems. Such concern is particularly evident on the northwestern coast, where approximately 426 shrimp farms operate, Sinaloa State being the primary producer.   文献综述

Shrimp aquaculture practices in Mexico vary from extensive to intensive production systems and depend on salinity, from hypersaline to brackish water regimes. Semintensive management is the dominant system (80%), characterized by shrimp postlarvae (PL) stocking densities of 60×10^3 to 2×10^5 PL/ha and yield of approximately 1000 to 2000 kg/ha. The intensive culture system is characterized by the combination of high initial stocking densities ($> 4 \times 10^5$ PL/ha) and feeding rates and the constant use of mechanical stirrers to ensure aerobic conditions. 背景信息

引言第三部分：

The paper presents a quantitative description of the dynamics of water quality variables monitored in influents and effluents during two consecutive growout cycles at four shrimp aquaculture farms (two semiintensive and two intensive aquaculture systems) located in the state of Sinaloa, Mexico. 研究内容

The aim of this research was to assess the influence of environmental factors and management practices on these water quality variables as well as to identify the most important relationship established among these key variables. 研究目的

(*Water Environment Research* Jan/Feb)

3.4 练习题

1. 用括号中动词的正确形式填空并指出各句表达的具体语篇功能。

(1) There are several important issues that _____ (not address).

(2) The rapid advances in computer software and hardware _____ (make) computing a growing and essential part of nearly every engineering discipline.

(3) The primary objectives of the investigation _____ (assess) the bridge's load-carrying capacity and compare this capacity with current standards of safety.

(4) A more integrated approach _____ (need) to complement existing simulation-based planning approaches.

(5) The work _____ (report) here is the first in a series aimed at developing automatic methods for the control of various parameters in drinking water _____ (intend) for human consumption.

(6) Over a period of several decades, wavelet analysis _____ (apply) to quite diverse fields.

(7) No studies on the performance of both irrigation systems are available, and the simulation of level furrows _____ (not attempt).

(8) The importance of programming competence _____ (remain) unchanged as one of the computing skills in civil engineering.

(9) Evaluation tests _____ (confirm) that the system that has been developed is even applicable to position detection in tunnels.

(10) The result _____ (not correspond) to a normal distribution.

(11) The present research _____ (demonstrate) how one might identify the sensors and control devices employed, build a design model, develop a controller, and evaluate a complete control system design.

(12) The next section briefly _____ (describe) the method of analysis and _____ (integrate) the theoretical model and its statistical tests.

(13) This system _____ (ensure) higher stability and greater precision in position detection than the existing system.

(14) Since the first observation of electrical conductivity in the compound, polymers _____ (receive) a great deal of attention both for their fundamental properties and their potential application.

(15) Very few equilibrium data on this ligand _____ (report), and the values of the equilibrium constants published _____ (differ) greatly, even for identical systems.

2. 按照引言的结构要素分析下列两篇引言(各分句已用阿拉伯数字标出)。

I

(1) Many of the suspension bridges built in the United States in the 19th Century are still in use today but were obviously designed for live loads quite different from the vehicular traffic they are subjected to today. (2) A good example is the John A. Roebling suspension bridge, completed in 1867, over the Ohio River between Covington, Kentucky, and Cincinnati, Ohio. (3) To continue using these historic bridges, it is necessary to evaluate their load-bearing capacity so that traffic loads are managed to ensure their continued safe operation. (4) Preservation of these historic bridges is important since they are regarded as national treasures.

(5) The unique structural style of suspension bridges permits longer span lengths, which are aesthetically pleasing but also add to the difficulties in performing accurate structural analysis. (6) Design of the suspension bridges built in the early 19th century was based on a geometrically linear theory with linear-elastic stress-strain behavior. (7) Such a theory is sufficiently accurate for shorter spans or for designing relatively deep, rigid stiffening systems that limit the deflections to a small fraction of the span length. (8) However, a geometrically linear theory is not well adapted to the design of suspension bridges with long spans, shallow trussed, or a large dead load. (9) A more exact theory is required that takes into account the deformed configuration of the structure.

(10) In modern practice, finite-element (FE) analysis is effective in performing the geometric nonlinear analysis of suspension bridges. (11) Geometric nonlinear theory can

include the nonlinear effects inherent in suspension bridges: cable sags, large deflections, and axial force and bending moment interaction with the bridge stiffness. (12) Two-dimensional or three-dimensional finite-element (FE) models with beam and truss elements are often used for both the superstructure and the substructure of cable-supported bridges.

(13) Another area where FE analysis has had a major impact regarding suspension bridge analysis is in predicting the vibration response of such bridges under wind, traffic, and earthquake loadings. (14) In addition, major efforts have been expended to predict the lateral, torsional, and vertical vibrations of suspension bridges to predict their dynamic behavior. (15) FE parametric studies have demonstrated the variation in the modal frequencies and shapes of stiffened suspension bridges.

(16) Structural evaluation using dynamics-based methods has become an increasingly utilized procedure for nondestructive testing. (17) A difficulty with dynamics-based methods is establishing an accurate FE model for the aging structure. (18) FE models typically provide dynamic performance predictions that exhibit relatively large frequency differences when compared with the experimental frequencies and, to a lesser extent, the models also predict differences in the modes of response. (19) These differences come not only from the modeling errors resulting from simplified assumptions made in modeling the complicated structures, but also from parameter errors due to structural damage and uncertainties in material and geometric properties. (20) Dynamics-based evaluation is therefore based on a comparison of the experimental modal analysis data obtained from in situ field tests with the FE predictions. (21) To improve the FE predictors, the FE model must realistically be updated (calibrated) to produce the experimental observed dynamic measurements. (22) Thus the scope of this study on the dynamic-based evaluation of the Roebling suspension bridge is composed of several tasks: FE modeling, modal analysis, in situ ambient vibration testing, FE model updating, and bridge capacity evaluation under live loading.

(23) This paper presents the results of the first two tasks in the dynamics-based evaluation scheme of the Roebling suspension bridge. (24) A 3D FE model is developed for the ANSYS commercial FE computer program. (25) All the geometric nonlinear sources discussed previously are included in the model. (26) A static dead-load analysis is carried out to achieve the deformed equilibrium configuration. (27) Starting from this deformed configuration, a modal analysis is performed to provide the frequencies and mode shapes that strongly affect the free vibration response of the bridge. (28) Parametric studies are performed to determine the significant material and structural parameters. (29) Results of the FE model analysis are compared with ambient vibration measurements in the accompanying paper. (30) This FE model, after being updated (calibrated) based on the experimental measurements, will serve as the baseline for the structural evaluation of the bridge. (31) The baseline structural evaluations provide important design information that will assist in the preservation of the Roebling suspension bridge, and furthermore, the

methodology developed in these two papers can be applied to wide range historic cable-supported bridges.

(*Journal of Bridge Engineering*)

II

(1) Software is becoming increasingly important and is being used in many critical applications, such as avionics, vehicle control system, medical systems, manufacturing, power systems, and sensor networks. (2) Meanwhile, software is also becoming increasingly complex—software is used to provide sophisticated features as well as to make the system robust to user errors and hardware failures; all of these make the state space of the software so large that it is difficult to have high confidence in the reliability, safety, and stability of the system. (3) Because of the increasing importance and complexity of such software applications, it is necessary to be able not only to achieve high quality, but also to demonstrate rigorously that high quality has in fact been achieved, so that we can have high confidence in the quality of the software prior to deploying it in the field.

(4) For these kinds of software systems, one viable approach is the "divide & conquer" method. (5) This encompasses two software engineering aspects, namely, development and certification:

- Development: decomposition of the software into smaller subsystems, each of which deals with a smaller state space.
- Certification: verification and validation of the properties of the software and analysis of the reliability and safety of the software.

(6) Various "divide & conquer" methods have been proposed, such as Aspect-Oriented Software Development (AOSD), Interface Grammar, Micro Protocol and Composite Protocol Technique, Protocol Projection method, and Sequence Diagram Specification method. (7) These will be reviewed in Section 5. (8) Basically, there are two potential limitations with existing decomposition methods:

- The decomposition process is manually intensive and not automated, i.e., they are based on the designer's experience and ability and, hence, can be error-prone.
- The system level properties, such as the overall system safety, stability, and reliability, cannot be inferred from the corresponding component level properties. Hence, conventional integration testing and verification of the entire system is still needed. For systems with very huge state spaces, it can be very costly to test them to a high degree of confidence and demonstrate that high quality has in fact been achieved.

(9) Considering these deficiencies, we present a new decomposition method that decomposes a system into simpler components, each of which can be seen as a specific aspect of the system that can be executed independently and produce some subset of the system behavior. (10) These components can be designed and implemented independently of each other. (11) Furthermore, these components can also be tested or verified by the

end-user independently of each other. (12) We refer to these components as IDEAL (Independently Developable End-user Assessable Logical) components. (13) The overall system properties, such as system safety, stability, and reliability, can be mathematically inferred from the properties of the individual IDEAL components so that integration testing and verification of the entire system is not needed. (14) Since each IDEAL component can be solved and validated in its restricted "view" of the system, it is easier to implement and verify each individual IDEAL component as compared with the task of implementing and verifying the entire system.

(15) Currently, the concept of an aspect in the area of AOSD refers mainly to crosscutting concerns among object modules. (16) Research in the area of AOSD has focused on the capture, separation, and composition of these crosscutting concerns with object modules. (17) Usually, aspects are not considered to be stand-alone design elements that can be executed and evaluated in isolation. (18) Our research extends the concept of "aspect" to encompass orthogonal end-user visible requirements of the system that correspond to some subset of the functionality (e. g., transitions) of the system. (19) We present an approach for designing a system based primarily on a set of stand-alone composable aspects rather than aspects that are subsumed within objects and procedures.

(20) Our decomposition method is also automated, meaning that a series of principles are given to help the designer decompose a system into IDEAL components. (21) These principles can be evolved to support automated tools.

(22) The rest of this paper is organized as follows: Section 2 presents the system model of the applications for which our decomposition method is intended. (23) Section 3 introduces the automated decomposition method. (24) Section 4 illustrates this decomposition method using a case study specified by the High-Integrity Systems group at Sandia National Labs, which involves the control of an enhanced version of the Bay Area Rapid Transit (BART) system. (25) The related work is presented in Section 5. (26) Section 6 summarizes the paper and outlines some research directions.

(IEEE Transactions on Software Engineering)

3. 用所给动词的正确形式填空。

A

| develop | exhibit | investigate | include | demonstrate | quantify |

This paper ____1___ the application of robust, nonlinear observation and control strategies, namely sliding mode observation and control (SMOC), to semiactive vehicle suspensions using a model reference approach. The vehicle suspension model ____2___ realistic nonlinearities in the spring and MR damper elements, and the reference model incorporates skyhook damping. Since full state measurement is difficult to achieve in practice, a sliding mode observer (SMO) that requires only suspension deflection as a measured input ___3___. The performance and robustness of SMC, SMO and SMOC ___4___ through comprehensive computer simulations. The results ___5___ tracking error between the plant and a skyhook reference model as a measure of performance, as skyhook models ___6___ desirable ride quality and handling performance in most case.

B

| conclude | remain | introduce | require | overcome |

Active vehicle suspension system ___1___ in the early 1970s to overcome the drawbacks of passive suspensions, namely the inherent tradeoff between ride quality and handling performance. Despite their published benefits, these systems ___2___ complex, bulky, and expensive and are not common options on production vehicles. Semiactive suspension ___3___ many these limitations, albeit with a reduction in achievable ride quality and handling performance, though some researchers ___4___ that this reduction is quite small. Semiactive suspensions can be considerably more cost effective, compact and functionally simple as they ___5___ only a variable damper and a few sensors to achieve adequate performance.

C

| propose | examine | devise | discuss | begin |

The aim of this paper ___1___ a more objective framework for general capabilities evaluation (GCE) so as to avoid any discrepancies in consultant pre-selection decisions. The paper ___2___ by summarizing the commonly used criteria for GCE. The importance of CPC ___3___, and any perceptual differences between the client and consultant groups ___4___. Finally, a multi-criteria model for consultant pre-selection ___5___.

D

| recognize | give | become | provide | make |

The rapid advances in computer software and hardware ___1___ engineers with powerful means of processing, storing, retrieving, sharing, and displaying data. These advances ___2___ computing a growing and essential part of nearly every engineering discipline. The effective use of computing in engineering ___3___ by many as the key to increased individual, corporate, and national productivity. Applications of computing technologies ___4___ engineers a means of rapid access to a wide variety of information and ways to model complex engineering systems. Computing technologies in areas such as data management, artificial intelligence, concurrent processing, networking, communications, and interactive computer graphics ___5___ prominent in engineering.

E

| be   introduce   incorporate   have   propose |

Armstrong and Frederick ___1___ a kinematic hardening rule containing a recall term which ___2___ the fading memory effect of the strain path and essentially makes the rule non-linear in nature. Also, the rule that ___3___ by them considers the anisotropy of the tension and compression curves. Chaboche et al. proposed a decomposed non-linear kinematic hardening model which ___4___ a superposition of several Armstrong-Frederick hardening rules. Each of these decomposed rules ___5___ their specific purposes.

4. 按照引言必需性结构要素缩写以下学术论文引言。

I

Fractal image coding is based on approximating an image by an attractor of a set of affine transforms, which was originally developed by Barnsley et al. in 1988. Subsequently, Jacquin implemented a block-based fractal compression algorithm using the partition iterated function System (PIFS), which is popularly known as fractal block coding. The encoding of each range block consists of finding the "best-pair" domain block within the domain block pool. The resulting fractal code consists of luminance offset and contrast scaling parameters, and location of the "best pair" domain block. To find the optimal bit allocation of fractal parameters, Tong et al. proposed substituting luminance offset with range block mean in the fractal code.

Because an image can be characterized by its fractal codes, the fractal codes can also be used as the image signature to retrieve an image from image databases. Based on this observation, several fractal-code based image retrieval (FCBIR) techniques have recently been proposed.

Zhang et al. have proposed an FCBIR technique where the fractal codes are used as the image index (henceforth referred to as FC technique). The authors considered two cases. In the first case, the query image size is identical to the candidate images in the database. In the second case, the query image is a part of the individual candidate images. Since the domain block pool of the query image is a subset of the domain block pool of a candidate image, the fractal code corresponding to the local domain block pool is different from that corresponding to the global domain block pool. To minimize the dissimilarity in fractal codes, the candidate images are segmented into blocks of different size and the blocks are arranged in a nona-tree (each node has nine branches). Fractal codes of each block are then obtained by searching the corresponding domain block pool, instead of the domain block pool of the entire candidate image. Although the FC technique provides fast retrieval, the corresponding fractal codes cannot be used to reconstruct the retrieved image.

A few researchers have used the features extracted from fractal codes as indices. Julie et al. proposed two major attributes as image indices: average of contrast scaling parameters, and the average of the luminance offsets. Although this technique has good indexing performance, the computational complexity is very high. Lasfar et al. have proposed a retrieval technique (henceforth referred to as the FDI technique) using the first decoding image (where iteration is initiated from the query image) as an image index. However, the computational complexity of this technique is very high, and the retrieval fails when the candidate image is a translated version of the query image.

The gray-scale histogram of gray or color pixels is known to have good indexing and retrieval performance while being computationally inexpensive. Schouten et al. extended this technique to the fractal domain. The authors highlight contrast scaling parameter and proposed using histogram of contrast scaling parameters as an image index (henceforth this technique is referred to as the HWQCS technique). Although the retrieval is very fast, this index does not provide a high retrieval rate.

The FC technique is based on direct match between the fractal codes (and is not based on match between statistical metrics), and hence it is not adapted for retrieval of homogeneous images. The HWQCS technique adopted statistical features; however, it highlights the contrast scaling parameter, while ignoring luminance offset. It should be noted that the affine transform from domain block into range block is determined by contrast scaling parameter and luminance offset.

Traditional fractal parameters have some inherent drawbacks. Luminance offset and the contrast scaling parameter both depend on the best-pair domain block, and are strongly correlated. Retrieval fails when the query image is a part of candidate images. To address this problem, we replace luminance offset with range block mean. This modification improves the performance of the FC technique by reducing the dissimilarity between the fractal codes of the query image and candidate images.

In this paper, we prove that the range block mean and contrast scaling parameters are independent. Based on this independence, we proposed four statistical indices utilizing the histograms of range block mean and contrast scaling parameters. In addition, we propose a hierarchical retrieval strategy to speed up retrieval based on the dc and ad component analysis. Histogram of range block means (relating to the dc component) is a good approximation to gray-scale histogram, and provides a retrieval rate similar to the retrieval rate provided by gray-scale histogram. On the other hand, visually different texture images with similar gray-scale histogram can be further discriminated by the joint histogram of range block mean and contrast scaling parameters. Hence, the proposed technique may be regarded as an improvement over traditional indexing techniques based on a gray-scale histogram.

The remainder of the paper is organized as follows: Section II reviews a few selected fractal block coding and indexing techniques. The proposed indices and retrieval method are described in Section III and IV. Experimental results on a texture image database are reported in Section V, which is followed by the conclusion.

(IEEE Transactions on Multimedia)

II

Heat-driven absorption cycles provide refrigeration/air-conditioning with environmentally friendly refrigerants, such as ammonia. The absorber is one of the critical components of such systems in terms of size, efficiency, and cost. The key features of an efficient design are high heat and mass transfer coefficients, and a large surface contact area. Other criteria of a good design are low-pressure drops in the liquid, vapor, and coolant regimes. The vapor flow mechanism divides absorbers into two broad categories, namely, those operating in falling film absorption mode and those in bubble absorption mode. The falling film mode over horizontal coolant tubes has been widely utilized in commercial absorption systems. The design accomplishes a low pressure drop on the vapor-side, but it has a low surface contact area and unstable liquid distribution. Numerous heat and mass transfer enhancement techniques like surface profiling/ modification, miniaturization, extended fins, and use of surfactants have been extensively analyzed and studied by researchers.

Techniques such as sand blasting, surface patterning, scratching, and surface oxidation have been used to improve the wetting characteristics of liquid film. The effect of porous surface on the enhancement of surface wettability was studies by Yang and Jou. Benzeguir et al. profiled the solution-side heat transfer surface by employing grooved and wire-wound tubes to generate large mixing waves. Miller and Perez-Blanco studied the effect of a solution-side tubular surface with pin fins, grooves, and twisted fins on the enhancement of mixing and uniformity of the falling film. Similar to the above concept of profiling the solution-side surface, Schwarzer et al. used spiral steps on the inner periphery of the tubes. In addition to the increase in fluid mixing, fins also act as obstructions in the vapor path that consequently induce turbulence in the flow. Constant curvature surfaces (CCS) were studied by Isshiki et al. for the purposed of forming a uniformly thick falling film. Surfactants are also utilized to enhance the mass transfer coefficient and wetting characteristics. The presence of surfactants causes a local variation in the surface tension, which in turn induces turbulence at the liquid-vapor interface. Much research has been devoted to quantifying and understanding the effect of the surfactants.

Another enhancement technique is the miniaturization of coolant section. It has already shown promising improvements in heat exchanger technology. Very high heat transfer coefficients can be achieved for microchannels, even in the laminar flow regime. In addition, the surface-to-volume ratio increases with the miniaturization of coolant sections. Garimella proposed the application of small-diameter coolant tubes in the falling film absorber. The experiments conducted by his group also confirmed that a very high absorption heat duty (16kW) could be accomplished in a compact absorber of a size 0.178m×0.178m×0.508m.

Recently, Islam et al. proposed a unique concept of periodically inverting the falling film while the liquid solution flows over the cooling surface. The liquid surface that was previously in contact with the cooled surface is in directly exposed to the vapor by inverting the film. This design not only increases in the mass flux, but also induces mixing due to shear forces. However, the effective liquid-coolant surface area was drastically reduced.

In the current work, a new design of a falling film absorber is proposed that could considerably reduce the absorber size. The proposed design is based on the fundamental characteristics of an efficient absorber design: large liquid-vapor interfacial area and good wetting characteristics. The design utilizes the unused vertical spacing between the coolant tubes to form the falling film, which consequently leads to an increase in the mass transfer area. The proposed design was numerically compared with a microchannel-based falling film absorber. As horizontal tube-type absorbers with small diameter coolant tubes are very compact, this analysis will help in comparing the proposed design with the current state-of-the-art absorber design.

(*Journal of Heat Transfer*)

Ⅲ

The World Parks Congress organized by the World Conservation Union (IUCN) is an important event in the protected area (PAs) field. It is held only every 10 years and seeks to provide direction for global initiatives for the subsequent decade. Some strange things happened as we approached the World Parks Congress in South Africa in September 2003. Publications of the IUCN began to characterize rice terraces, potato fields, Hyde Park and extractive reserves as "protected areas". A paper that was intended to help set the agenda for the Congress by the former head of the World Commission on Protected Areas (WCPA) of the IUCN, called for a "new paradigm" for protected area, the characteristics of which would see "new, more people-focused protected areas legislation" as well as "there-engineering" of protected areas people; the re-education of politicians and the public so they understand the new model of protected areas; and the reorientation of development assistance policies so as to integrate protected areas into poverty reduction strategies.

The opening plenary sessions at the Congress featured several speakers who advocated for IUCN protected area categories Ⅴ (protected landscape) and Ⅵ (managed resource areas) as the main focus for protected area activity in the future. The IUCN Bulletin summarizing the Congress declared "A new era for protected areas", an article in it stating "by the time we met in Durban it was evident that a wholly new paradigm of a protected area, and of its managements, had emerged".

The issue is of more than semantic interest; international treaties such as the Convention on Biological Diversity require signatory nations to establish PA systems as a response to the erosion of wild biodiversity (the CBD identifies domesticated and cultivated species as a subset of biodiversity, which are the focus of other conservation measures but not protected areas, see article 9, 10). This is the main purposed of PAs. However, under the new categories and supported by the "new paradigm", PAs are being recast as tools for social planning and income generation. The amount of land in PAs is rising rapidly, but we suggest these new directions compromise their effectiveness as tools for the conservation of wild biodiversity. Furthermore, the Seventh Conference of the Parties of the CBD, dealing specifically with the role of protected areas in biodiversity conservation urged member countries to adopt a "single international classification system for protected areas" (United Nations Environment Programme) and welcomed the efforts of IUCN in this regard. This is a sound direction, but it also emphasizes the need to have a thorough and open examination of the category system. IUCN has foreseen this need and a useful set of background papers were generated on the topic prior to the World Parks Congress and recently consolidated in a report. However, few conservation scientists or conservationists seem to be aware of the implications of the directions that have emerged regarding PA classification or the new paradigm. The purpose of this paper is to examine the new paradigm, its relationship to the IUCN PA category system and its implications for protected areas and wild biodiversity.

The paper opens with a clarification of PA purpose and discusses the IUCN PA categories, particularly categories Ⅴ and Ⅵ. It then proposes that these categories distort the meaning of PA and discusses the negative implications of the new paradigm for wild biodiversity. The paper closes with a proposed solution of reclassifying protected areas to include only those focused on wild biodiversity and reclassifying IUCN category Ⅴ and Ⅵ PAs as sustainable development areas.

(*Environmental Conservation*)

Ⅳ

Cylindrical structure consisting of eccentric layers are a common geometric form in many fields, ranging from biological structures such as bones and blood vessels, to telecommunication infrastructure such as cables and optical fibres, to underground pipelines, and to many other mechanical and civil structures in almost all sizes. Efforts in analyzing wave scattering characteristics by such structures have been relatively recent, compared to the long history of studies on sound and wave propagation. In 1974, Shaw and Tai first formulated the acoustic scattering by a two-layer eccentric cylinder using the boundary integral method. It was later extended to elastic longitudinal and shear wave problems. The normal mode expansion method was used for electromagnetic waves and the diffusion of neutrons in a nuclear reactor. By that time, approximate results were obtained by using a perturbation method for small eccentricities. The perturbation method remains a useful method for approximate solutions. More recently, exact numerical results have been obtained. In addition, Danila et al. used a generalized Debye series expansion to describe the physical process by reflection and transmission coefficients for each normal mode. Kishk et al. formulated the problem of scattering of electromagnetic waves by a scatterer of an arbitrary number of layers. Ioannidou et al. formulated the problem of scattering of electromagnetic waves by multiple scatterers enclosed within a cylindrical enclosure and by multiple eccentric multilayer scatterers enclosed by an eccentrically stratified cylinder.

The author's interest in this topic stems from the report of a new mechanism for band gap formation in phononic crystals made of silicone-coated lead balls. The new band gap is found at a frequency range about one order of magnitude lower than the one formed by the lattice structure. The mechanism is attributed to resonance between the springy silicone coating and the massive lead balls. The author investigated the scattering of elastic anti-plane shear wave (SH wave) by concentric scatterers and confirmed that such resonance also exists in two-dimensional problem. A simple model was established to predict the resonance frequency. Furthermore, a similarly low frequency resonance is shown to exist at another extreme when the coating is extremely heavy compared to other constituents. Recently, a similar resonance mechanism for electromagnetic waves has been utilized to construct artificial materials (meta-materials) with negative refractive index. From these conclusions, we therefore speculate that eccentricity in the coating might introduce additional mechanisms for tuning the resonance frequency.

In this paper, scattering of an elastic SH wave by an eccentrically layered cylindrical scatterer is studied. The analysis uses a novel multiple-scattering approach based on the recognition that multiple scattering occurs in multilayered scatterers. This approach has been used by the author in an earlier paper to analyze a concentric layered scatterer. The solution procedure follows the physical process as the wave interacts with various interfaces in the scatterer. It has been shown that the solution procedure is analytically exact, and is suitable for all types of waves.

Without loss of generality, the configuration considered in this paper consists of a bounded scatterer embedded in an unbounded medium. Assuming the unbounded medium is homogeneous and linearly elastic, and the scatterer is either homogeneous and linearly elastic, or rigid, or void, such that the problem is linear.

(*The Quarterly Journal of Mechanics and Applied Mathematics*)

3.5 相关阅读

1. Supplementary Reading Material 1

Introduction, as a genre, has conventionally been understood as a piece of discourse which introduces other forms of lengthy discourse, be it a research article, a project report, a laboratory report or even a student essay. Its communicative function is quite clear, but the way it is treated in a particular context depends largely on the requirements of the longer discourse it introduces; sometimes the subject discipline will also affect the way it is treated, as will, also, the organizational constraints imposed by the genre in question, particularly in the case of student lab reports and essays, which are generally written in direct response to the requirements made by the department or the teacher concerned.

2. Supplementary Reading Material 2

Introductions are known to be troublesome, and nearly all academic writers admit to having more difficulty with getting started on a piece of academic writing than they have with its continuation. The opening paragraphs somehow present the writer with an unnerving wealth of options: decisions have to be made about the amount and type of background knowledge to be included; decisions have to be made about an authoritative versus a sincere stance; decisions have to be made about the winsomeness of the appeal to the readership; and decisions have to be made about the directness of the approach. If we add to the above brief catalogue the assumption that first impressions matter (especially in an era of exponentially expanding literature). Then we are not surprised to note that over the last 10 years or so there has been growing interest in the introductory portions of texts.

One possible approach is to view research article introductions as encapsulated problem-solution texts. This, for instance, is the position adopted by Zappen who argues that researchers in their writing need continuously to address the context of the intellectual discipline wherein they are located. More specifically, the researcher addresses the goals, current capacities, problems, and criteria of evaluation that derive from the operation within that discipline.

3. Supplementary Reading Material 3

How to Write an Effective Introduction

Introduction

An introduction to an essay is brief, coherent, logical and stimulating, which puts the reader in a receptive mood. It is like a first impression—you only get one chance to draw the reader in. If the first two to three sentences do not catch your attention, will you continue to read on? It's unlikely! Without a strong introduction, you will turn the page to the next article, or surf to the next site, or pick up the next proposal. Therefore, you should take special care to create the best first impression that you can by writing an effective introduction. The purpose of this article is to help those embarking on research to communicate effectively through introduction writing, and to improve their chances of getting a paper published.

Problems in Introduction Writing

There are many problems in introduction writing. The five problems as follows should be avoided.

- Key points don't stand out. Many authors write long paragraphs to explain the background and the research process, spread out a lot of materials which have nothing to do with the paper and neglect the real aim of introduction.
- Not give out the research statement all over the world.
- Introduction is similar with abstract.
- Confuse introduction with conclusion and not coordinate with each other. Introduction is to awaken the reader's interest and prepare the reader to understand the paper, to convince the reader that this study is necessary, while the conclusion is to summarize the views in the article.
- Use charts, formulas, and illustrations in the introduction.

Content of Introduction

- Statement of the problem.
- Significance of the problem.
- What is known, what is not known or controversial?
- Statement of the question.
- References.

Rules of Introduction Writing

- Introduction just makes a redirection function, thus a 2000-word essay would have an introduction somewhere between 160 and 200 words; a 3500-word report between 290 and 350 words. An introduction should be no shorter than one-twelfth and no longer than one-tenth of the total assignment.
- Introduction should be clear and brief, use fewer words and express exact meaning. Don't give your reader too much content—give just enough to place the key issue of your assignment in its content.
- Charts, formulas, illustration should not appear in the introduction.
- Give vivid hypothesis in the introduction. A hypothesis is a specific statement or prediction. It describes in concrete terms what you expect to happen in your study. It is always a super-topic sentence (in present tense), sometimes it states as objective or logical from the background.
- The thesis statement must be given out. The thesis statement is always separated

from the rest of the introduction under the heading Aim (or Purpose) of the essay. It is usual to put the thesis statement at the end of the introduction, but it can sometimes be placed at the beginning. Don't put it in the middle of the introduction. The thesis statement often begins with expressions like: "This report examines…"; "This essay will discuss…"; "This article demonstrates…". We recommend that you adopt this strategy, especially if you are an inexperienced writer. That, you won't forget to put the thesis statement into your introduction, and your reader has a clear idea of what the focus will be.

- A simple structure should be kept. An effective introduction is one that begins with a very general statement about the subject, and then gradually narrows down to the specific thesis statement. The pattern is shown below: general statement about the subject, beginning the focus onto the topic, becoming more specific.
- Personal comment such as "I think that such-and-such" or "In my opinion, such-and-such" should be avoided.

Typical Steps in Writing Introduction

There are ten steps in developing an effective Introduction. However, since every journal is different, it is important that you look at papers in your targeted journals to determine whether they use all of these steps.

- Begin the Introduction by proving a concise background account of the problems studied.
- State the objective of the investigation. Your research objective is the most important part of the introduction.
- Establish the significance of your work: Why was there a need to conduct the study?
- Introduce the reader to the pertinent literature. Do not give a full history of the topic. Only quote previous work having direct bearing on the present problem.
- Clearly state your hypothesis, the variables investigated, and concisely summarize the methods used.
- Define any abbreviations or specialized terms.
- Provide a concise discussion of the results and findings of other studies so that the reader understands the big picture.
- Describe some of the major findings presented in your manuscript and explain how they contribute to the larger field of research.
- State the principal conclusions derived from your results.
- Identify any questions left unanswered and any new questions generated by your study.

Conclusion

We have talked about the chief problems in writing introduction, explained the significance of the introduction, given out the effective methods and rules to help the author write a good introduction. However, it is certain that the list can go on as everyone owns his or her experience and further study deepens. In a word, an introduction should be no shorter than one-twelfth and no longer than one-tenth of the total assignment. Remember that this is only a rule of thumb. There is no absolute rule about length. Just be sensible about it and you will write an effective introduction.

4. Supplementary Reading Material 4

Sample 1

An important issue in pattern recognition is the effect of insufficient samples available for training in classification accuracy. It is well known that when the ratio of the number of training samples to the number of the feature dimensionality is small, the estimates of the statistical model parameters are not accurate, and therefore the classification results may not be satisfactory. This problem is especially significant in offline signature verification, where the lack of sufficient signature samples from each writer for training is prevailing. One reason for the difficulty is attributable to the private and confidential nature of the signatures. Another reason is that human handwritings vary from time to time. It is desirable to collect the signature from a signer over an extended period of weeks or months instead of collecting all samples in one session, and this adds to the difficulty of obtaining a large number of samples from a person. In any case, usually only a limited number of samples can be obtained to train an offline signature verification system, which further makes offline signature verification a formidable task.

A considerable amount of effort has been devoted to designing a classifier particular to small sample size situation. To avoid unreliable estimation of statistical parameters due to a small number of training samples, nonparametric classifiers such as a nearest neighbor classifier, may be believed to be effective. The decision of nearest neighbor only involves the computation of pairs of feature vectors. However, the offline signature verification is usually considered to be a specific case of the typical two-class classification problem, with training samples available only to model the classifier. There is no information about forgeries available to estimate class statistics before the signature verification system has been implemented. This situation causes various kinds of distance-based threshold classifiers to be widely adopted in signature verification. Hence, nonparametric approaches are not suitable for offline signature verification application. For threshold classifier based on statistical distance such as Mahalanobis distance, class distributions for an individual writer are modeled by a set of statistics from training samples. The class statistics are mean vector and covariance matrix of Gaussian distribution assumption. The maximum likelihood estimator is usually used to estimate such statistics. However, estimation error can be a significant problem for the limited amount of training samples, which renders the estimation of the statistics unreliable. Moreover, when the number of training samples is less than the dimensionality of the feature space, the sample covariance matrix is singular and its inverse does not exist, so the Mahalanobis distance cannot be computed.

There are several ways to overcome the problem of estimation error for class statistics in the case of small training sample size. These techniques are categorized into three groups: (1) dimensionality reduction by feature extraction and feature selection; (2) regularization of sample covariance matrix; and (3) structurization of a true covariance matrix described by a small number of parameters. Feature extraction employs feature transformation to reduce the feature dimensionality to save computing cost and avoid the curse of dimensionality, whereas feature selection does the same job by selecting a subset of the original feature set that performs the best classification. However, the between-class scatter matrix as selection criterion used by these approaches cannot be computed due to the special characteristics of signature verification that training samples come from genuine class only. Hence, these approaches are not applicable in the study to estimate stable class statistics. The orthogonal transformation for the purpose of correlation reduction among matrix elements is used to diagonalize covariance matrix by decreasing the number of statistics. However, correlation information among features may be useful to provide discriminatory information for classification. Moreover, the class statistics estimation error is still significant in the situation of small training sample size, even if the feature dimensionality has been reduced.

In this paper, we proposed two approaches to reduce statistics estimation error in respect to small training sample size in offline signature verification. The first approach employs an elastic distortion model applied to pairs of genuine signature patterns to artificially generate additional training samples. The training set used to estimate statistics includes the original genuine samples and the generated samples that are more representative of the true sampling distribution. This study augments contents by background discussion and detailed algorithms description. Performance comparison with other methods to produce artificial training samples has also been presented. Another approach is to adopt a matrix regularization technique to sample covariance matrix dealing with the specific one-class problem in offline signature verification. A ridge-like estimator is used to add some constant values to diagonal elements of the sample covariance matrix. The estimator overcomes the problem of inverse of an ill-conditioned covariance matrix and obtains stabilized estimation. Experimental results showed that matrix regularization technique also produced improved verification accuracy, although it was not better than additional sample approach. Both methods are implemented with a set of peripheral feature. The reason to adopt peripheral features that describe outline and internal structure of the signature patterns is that they have been proven to provide more discriminatory capability than other local and global signature representations for our database. The system flowchart for offline signature verification to cope with the sparse data problem incorporated with peripheral features and Mahalanobis distance classifier is illustrated.

Sample 2

Sensitivity analysis is an important method for solving various optimization problems in transportation systems. Efficient computational algorithms for sensitivity analysis of the multinominal logit stochastic user equilibrium model have been provided by Clark and Watling which can deal with more general SUE models including the probit model.

The purpose of this work is to develop effective sensitivity analysis methods for solving various optimization problems in a combined transport system consisting of an automobile road network along with a physically separate public transit network, e. g., a railway or subway network. The explicit treatment of transit network is important in transportation system optimization problems. In particular, due to the complex cost structure of transit system, there is a need to explicitly formulate its cost functions in order to set road tolls and transit fares that is optimal from the social welfare point of view. In this paper, we assume that the supplier of the transit service is a zero-profit firm. We also assume that the subsidies for part of the fixed cost for the construction of the transit and an operational cost from the public sector are given in lump sum and the rest of the costs are shared by the passengers so that the firm breaks even. Even in this simplified framework, there are many factors that make up the complexity of the structure of the cost incurred by transit users. On the one hand, in a metropolitan area, congestion is usually a dominating factor that causes external diseconomies for the transit users. On the other hand, in rural regions where the passenger flows are far less than the potential capacity of the transit system, the increase of passengers brings about extra profit to the supply side of the transit service, which may be re-invested for accomplishing a higher frequency operation schedule, thus shortening the waiting time in using transit and decrease the general cost of the passengers. Such a case involves external economies or economies of scale. Another well-studied factor accounting for the economics of scale is that the fixed cost for construction of a transit system, even after being partially subsidized, is still very large. If the transit service is offered under a break-even constraint, as is assumed in this work, increased passengers will lead to a lower fare because they share the fixed and variable service cost.

In this paper we provide sensitivity analysis methods for two kinds of combined transport systems. The first is the case where a transit network with general topology exists along with the road network and both networks are congested, that is, the cost incurred by passenger is a function increasing absolutely with the passenger flow on each link in each network. An efficient link-based sensitivity analysis method is proposed for computing the derivatives of road link vehicle flows and transit link passenger flows with respect to the link parameters. Under the congestion assumptions, the equilibrium traffic flow assignment problem has a unique solution. The proposed sensitivity analysis method always works for such an equilibrium. The results are presented in Section 2. The second case is a system with a road network and transit lines directly connecting Origin-

Destination (O-D) pairs. The performance function of each transit line may have external diseconomies caused by congestion, as well as economies of scale. In such a case, economies of scale on the transit, the modal split and traffic assignment problem involves the difficulty of singularity. For this case, the sensitivity analysis algorithm is also provided and conditions are examined under which the sensitivity analysis can be applied. These results are presented in Section 3. An example is given in Section 4 for demonstrating the effectiveness of proposed sensitivity analysis algorithm for solving the optimal pricing problem in the transport system with the road network and O-D-specific transit lines which may have economies of scale. A social utility for the combined transportation system is introduced based on random utility theory. The example shows that besides the well-known marginal cost pricing scheme, there are pricing schemes that optimize the social utility. Some related problems are described in Section 5.

Sample 3

Active vehicle suspension systems were introduced in the early 1970s to overcome the drawbacks of passive suspension, namely the inherent tradeoff between ride quality and handling performance. Despite their published benefits, these systems remain complex, bulky, and expensive and are not common options on production vehicles. Semiactive suspension overcome many of these limitations, albeit with a reduction in achievable ride quality and handling performance, though some researchers have concluded that this reduction is quite small. Semiactive suspensions can be considerably more cost effective, compact and functionally simple as they require only a variable damper and a few sensors to achieve adequate performance.

The recent introduction of commercial magnetorheological (MR) fluid dampers has enabled high-bandwidth, low-power control of suspension damping forces with very few mechanical parts. These semiactive components contain suspensions of micron-sized, magnetizable particles in oil-based fluid. In the presence of magnetic fields, these fluid particles become aligned with the field, dramatically increasing the fluid viscosity and effective damping. Recently, Carerra has introduced MagneShockTM and Delphi Automotive Systems has introduced MagnerideTM, both using MR fluid technology to enable semiactive damping adjustments at frequencies up 1000Hz.

The performance of semiactive suspension systems relies heavily on real-time control strategies. Early research focused primarily on linear techniques, such as optimal control and skyhook control. However, vehicle suspensions contain dynamic nonlinearities associated with springs and dampers, sliding friction in joints and nonlinear kinematics which significantly affect ride quality and handling performance. Vehicle suspensions are also subject to parameter variations (i.e., changes in damping and stiffness characteristics over extended time periods) that adversely affect the robustness of many algorithms.

For these reasons, recent semiactive control research has focused more on nonlinear control techniques. Gordon and Best extended previous nonlinear optimal designs to semiactive suspensions and incorporated dynamic parameter optimization. Hedrick and Sohn linearized the vehicle dynimics about an equilibrium point and applied skyhook control to a semiactive MacPherson strut suspension. Henry and Zeid derived a suboptimal nonlinear control law, but did not consider spring and damper nonlinearities. Considerable research effort has concentrated on fuzzy logic, neural networks and artificial intelligence techniques. The primary advantages of these approaches are that complete knowledge of the plant dynamics may not be required, and hence nonlinearities may be incorporated easily. The primary drawbacks of such methods include the ad hoc nature of controller synthesis and absence of robustness guarantees.

Sliding mode control (SMC) is a highly effective nonlinear and robust control strategy. It is insensitive to unmodelled dynamics and parametric uncertainties and has been used effectively in automotive, aerospace and robotic applications. Kim and Ro developed SMC for a nonlinear active suspension system and compared it to a self-tuning controller. Results showed that SMC significantly improved robust tracking performance when vehicle parameters changed. Alleyne and Hedrick used SMC for a nonlinear actuator in an active vehicle suspension system. Yokoyama et al. demonstrated the effectiveness of SMC for MR semiactive suspension systems using a model following approach.

This paper investigates the application of robust, nonlinear observation and control strategies, namely sliding mode observation and control (SMOC), to semiactive vehicle suspensions using a model reference approach. The vehicle suspension model includes realistic nonlinearities in the spring and MR damper elements, and the reference model incorporates skyhook damping. Since full state measurement is difficult to achieve in practice, a sliding mode observer (SMO) that requires only suspension deflection as a measured input is developed. The performance and robustness of SMC, SMO and SMOC are demonstrated through comprehensive computer simulations. The results quantify tracking error between the plant and skyhook reference model as a measure of performance, as skyhook models exhibit desirable ride quality and handling performance in most cases.

第4章 结论

4.1 概述

结论是论文主要论点的总结和复述,是论文实质内容的提炼和浓缩。尽管各类科研论文正文论述部分的格式有所差异,但绝大多数学术论文作者一般都会采用结论作为研究论文的收尾,并试图通过结论向读者重申或强化自己的表述意向。

4.2 构成要素

结论应概括、总结论文中所提及的内容,但不单纯是正文中各段小结的简单重复。总体来说,结论主要由三部分构成:

1. 总结与回顾

总结与回顾即总结、回顾论文各部分的主要内容。参见下例:

例1 **We have introduced a novel design methodology which** facilitates design-for-EC and post-processing to enable EC with minimal perturbation. **Initially**, as a synthesis preprocessing step, the original specification is augmented with additional design constraints which ensure flexibility for future correction. **Upon alteration of the initial design, a novel** post-processing **technique achieves** the desired functionality with near-minimal perturbation of the optimized design.

笔者介绍了一种全新的……设计方法……。起初,……。对最初设计修订后,新的……技术实现了……

例2 **A new concept of** forming a falling film in between the horizontal coolant tubes by a flow guidance medium like a mesh **is presented. The new design is numerically analyzed and compared to** the horizontal tube-type falling film absorber.

论文提出了……的新概念,对新设计进行了数值分析,并对比了……

2. 讨论与评述

讨论与评述即讨论、评述该论文的研究意义。

参见下例:

例1 **The proposed model is beneficial to** municipalities and construction/maintenance contractors, **and can work as a powerful supplement to** infrastructure management systems.

所述模式有助于……,……是……的有力补充。

例 2 **The new design will** induce through mixing of the liquid film while it flows alternatively over the mesh and coolant tubes. **Also, the simplicity of the concept makes it viable to** incorporate it in existing falling film absorbers.

新的设计将……。同样,该理念的简化将使……具有可行性。

3. 建议与展望

建议与展望即对现阶段研究的不足之处提出建议,或对该课题未来的发展趋势及进一步研究的可能性予以展望。

参见下例:

例 1 **Some related themes worth further studying are listed as follows**:…

一些具有进一步研究价值的相关主题列举如下:……

例 2 **The use of** scenario-planning in the context of Mexico City air-quality-management project currently underway, in which the first two writers of this paper are involved, **will hopefully** help to answer some of these questions. **However, there is hope that others might** undertake field applications to help see how planning agencies can adapt the proposed approach and how the approach might compare in use and ultimate results with other approaches.

……的使用有望……。然而,其他研究人士也有望……

4.3 写作范式

4.3.1 总结与回顾的写作范式(见表 4-1)

表 4-1 总结与回顾的写作范式

In this paper/thesis,	the author/writer	argues that…	该论文中,笔者认为……
		concludes that…	该论文中,笔者下定结论……
		finds that…	该论文中,笔者发现……
		points out that…	该论文中,笔者指出……
	…	has been investigated. The major conclusions are:…	该论文研究了……,得出的主要结论有:……
To summarize,	the article/paper	concludes that…	总之,本论文结论可归结为……
		provides that…	总之,本文提供了……
		shows that…	总之,本文展示了……
In summary,	the conclusion/result	is that…	总之,结论/结果为……
		indicates that…	总之,结论/结果表明……
In sum,	it	is proved that…	总之,该论文/研究证明了……
	we	have explored…	总之,笔者探究了……
		have examined…	总之,笔者验证了……
		have introduced…	总之,笔者引入了……
On the basis of the above…,	we can see that …		基于……,笔者发现……
From…,	we should say that …		从……中,笔者可以认定……
From the above…,	we may come to the conclusion that …		如上文所述,笔者可得出……的结论

参见下例：

例1 **We introduced a new** bearing fault detection and diagnosis **scheme** based on hidden Markov modeling (HMM) of vibration signals. In this new scheme, HMM models were trained to present various bearing conditions. These models were then used to detect both single-and multiple-bearing faults based on the model probabilities. The new scheme was tested with experimental data collected from an accelerometer measuring the vibration from the drive-end ball bearing of an induction motor-driven mechanical system.

笔者介绍了一种全新的……设计方案……

例2 **In this paper**, the effect of cross-sectional shapes and geometric and loading imperfections on the behavior of FRP-confined columns **has been investigated**. **The major conclusions are**：…

该论文研究了……，得出的主要结论有：……

4.3.2 讨论与评述的写作范式（见表4-2）

表4-2 讨论与评述的写作范式

The presented experimental results validate …	论文所陈述的实验结果为……提供了充分依据
The proposed model is beneficial to …	文中提议的模式有益于……
… could make a major contribution to …	……对……会有重大贡献
… is of paramount importance	……是极为重要的
… the system has the potential to be used to accurately control …	该系统对于精确掌控……极具潜力
… making it easy to …	……便于……
Although our work is far from complete, it does provide a general methodological framework for dealing with …	尽管此项研究还远非尽善尽美，但对于处理……却实实在在地提出了一个总体的方法框架
As more and more clients are aware of the importance of …, … is indispensable	随着越来越多的客户意识到……的重要性，……将变得不可或缺

参见下例：

例1 **As a key contribution, we highlighted** the constraint manipulation technique which enables reduction of an arbitrary EC problem into its corresponding classical synthesis problem. **Consequently**, traditional synthesis algorithms can be used to enable flexibility and perform local alterations. **The presented experimental results validate** the correctness and cost effectiveness of our approach.

……的主要贡献在于笔者凸显了……。因此，……所陈述的实验结果为……提供了充分依据。

例2 **As more and more clients are aware of the importance of** consultant selection, **the development of a more** informed framework for evaluating consultants **is indispensable**. **The GCE model outlined in this paper would help improve** the transparency of this kind of decision **and should be welcomed by** the clients and consultants.

随着越来越多的客户意识到……的重要性。研发一种更为……的模式就显得尤为必要。文中所概述的……模式有助于改善……，因而将受到……的青睐。

例3 This letter has proven that the residual source redundancy **effectively contributes to**

error correction, acting like a channel code redundancy.

……有助于……

例 4 For situations such as exit on the high traffic density Birmingham interstate system, a quality construction job with a durable material done in a rapid manner **is of paramount importance.**

……是极为重要的。

例 5 It is automatically synthesized out of a simple user-provided description, **making it easy to** adapt VPC4 to other trace formats and to tune it.

……使得……易于……

例 6 **Although our work is far from complete**, it does provide a general methodological **framework for dealing with** the two-fold non-convexity in optimal design and management of transportation system.

尽管此项研究还远非尽善尽美，但对于处理……却实实在在地提出了一个总体的方法框架。

例 7 **Evaluation tests have confirmed that the system** that has been developed **is even applicable** to position detection in tunnels and that **the system has the potential to be used to accurately control** the carbody of tilting trains.

评估测试确定该系统还可适用于……，该系统对于精确掌控……极具潜力。

4.3.3 建议与展望的写作范式（见表 4-3）

表 4-3 建议与展望的写作范式

It should also address the analysis of …	同样，应重视对……的分析
Future work should include …	后续研究应涉及……
Some related themes worth further studying are listed as follows:…	一些具有进一步研究价值的相关主题列举如下：……
The results of this research should be directly …	该研究的结果将直接（用于）……
It is expected that … will continue to play a role in …	可以预见，……将继续起着……作用

参见下例：

例 1 **Future work should include** the analysis of the transition from sliding to rolling and applications to technological problems. **It should also address the analysis of** the three-dimensional problem (spherical case) for sliding and rolling motions.

后续研究应涉及……。同样，应重视对……的分析。

例 2 **The results of this research should be directly transferable to** actual semiactive vehicle suspension implementations.

该研究成果将直接转化应用于……

例 3 **It is expected that** equation solvers and databases **will continue to play a role in future** civil engineering computing applications.

可以预见，……在未来将继续发挥……作用。

4.3.4 范文分析

本节选出两篇英文学术论文的结论全文，通过分析范文，可以清晰地看到学术论文结论的结构特征和语言特征。

1）范文一

Conclusion

A new concept of forming a falling film in between the horizontal coolant tubes by a flow guidance medium like a mesh **is presented. The new design is numerically analyzed and compared** to the horizontal tube-type falling film absorber. 总结与回顾

The advantage of increasing the mass transfer area by forming the falling film between the nonutilized vertical spacing **is evident from the numerical results. The proposed design is more compact and efficient than** the falling film absorber based on small diameter coolant tubes. **A size reduction of** about 25% **is possible** for the operating conditions considered. **The new design will induce** through mixing of the liquid film while it flows alternatively over the mesh and coolant tubes. **Also, the simplicity of the concept makes it viable to** incorporate it in existing falling film absorbers. 讨论与评述

However, several flow mechanisms associated with the flow over the horizontal tubes and fabric/mesh **are not considered** in order to realize a numerical model. For example, the effect of the fabric/mesh on the larger residence time of the falling film, lack of adiabatic adsorption in the droplets, fin effect of the metallic mesh, wettability enhancement, prevention of the satellite droplets, etc. **are neglected in the current analysis. A complete analysis of** the complex heat and mass transfer processes coupled with a flow analyses of falling film **is not available in the literature. In addition, the current literature also lacks** numerical and experimental flow analysis of a falling film over an irregular mesh. **An experimental study is currently being conducted by the authors to** compare the performance of the proposed and horizontal tube-type falling film absorber designs. **It will help in** considering the complex phenomena that were unaccounted for in this numerical scheme. **However, this is the preliminary attempt** to analyze the proposed design with the currently available numerical models. **There is no consensus among researchers regarding** the existence of a dominant resistance to mass transfer in either the liquid or vapor phase. The mass transfer resistance **is quite often neglected** in either phase to simplify the numerical models. In this model, **we have attempted to avoid the above mentioned controversy by considering** the heat and mass resistances in both the liquid and vapor phases. 建议与展望

(*Journal of Heat Transfer*)

2）范文二
Conclusion

We presented a novel approach to privacy where only gaining confidence in a sensitive fact is illegal, while losing confidence is allowed. 　　总结与回顾

We showed that this relaxation **is significant and permits many more** queries **than with well-known approaches. In exchange,** this gave us an opportunity to relax prior knowledge assumptions beyond current standards. 　　讨论与评述

Our hope is that work in this direction will help bridge the gap between theoretical soundness and practical usefulness of privacy frameworks. **One possible future goal is to obtain a better understanding of** the families of sets and distributions that arise in practice, and to understand whether they admit efficient privacy tests. **Another goal is to apply the new frameworks to** online (proactive) auditing, which will require the modeling of a user's knowledge about the auditor's query-answering strategy. 　　建议与展望

（*Journal of ACM*）

4.4　练习题

1. 分析下面两篇结论的构成要素。

I

The paper examined the GCE criteria pertinent to the pre-selection of engineering consultants. Through a series of interviews, these criteria were classified into four broad categories viz., technical capabilities, management capabilities, financial capabilities, and quality attitude. A questionnaire survey was conducted, which revealed that technical capabilities were considered the most crucial category by the clients who were pre-selecting their consultants. Quality attitude was conceived by the clients as having the least impact when evaluating consultants' general capabilities. More efforts should be directed to ensure that the technical capabilities of consultants are evaluated carefully and objectively.

Detailed investigations were also conducted to examine the importance of the 28 CPC identified, and the results revealed that the view of the clients and consultants were fairly consistent. This indicated that a universal set of weightenings could be applied for evaluating consultants' GCE. There were four criteria where the consultants rated not as important as the client group though. These criteria included the number of professional, technical and administrative staff, time management system, amount of time overrun in designing previous project, and any adverse audit report received. Consultants had underestimated the importance of delivering the project at the quality standard and time frame that the client would like to achieve. These could affect the score they would receive at the pre-selection period.

A multi-criteria model for GCE was proposed in this paper. The weightenings at different levels, which include the main category, sub-category, and CPC, were computed according to the data collected from the client group through the survey on the importance of criteria collected through the questionnaire. Clients can simply adopt the weightings in designing their standardized pre-selection checklist. Therefore, the only thing for the evaluation team to do is to assign a score for each criterion according to the information supplied by the clients. Based on the formulae proposed in this paper, a final score can be computed for each consultant, and those who have received higher scores can be regarded as more capable consultants. Some of the criteria used cannot be easily quantified which may give rise to subjective evaluation by different assessors. In order to further improve the pre-selection process, an objective means of scoring is required, and this important issue is being examined by the authors. As more and more clients are aware of the importance of consultant selection, the development of a more informed framework for evaluating consultants is indispensable. The GCE model outlined in this paper would help improve the transparency of this kind of decision and should be welcomed by clients and consultants.

(Engineering, Construction and Architectural Management)

Ⅱ

In this paper, the effect of cross-sectional shapes and geometric and loading imperfections on the behavior of FRP-confined columns has been investigated. The major conclusions are:

- The FRP confinement is most effective for columns of a circular cross section. For noncircular cross sections, although the stiffness of the columns remains close to that of circular ones, the ultimate strain of the column decreases. As a result, the ultimate strength also decreases. The failure of concentrically loaded noncircular column takes place at the corners.
- The maintenance of a minimum corner radius is of great importance for noncircular column. A finite-element study has been presented to determine the minimum corner radius that is necessary. It has been found that at a 15mm corner radius, the hoop stress concentration in FRP is negligible.
- A modification of the confinement factor has been proposed to model noncircular columns. The factor determines the diameter of an equivalent noncircular column.
- The effect of geometric imperfection is included as a modification factor based on the slenderness ratio of the columns.
- Due to loading imperfections, it is found that the ultimate load reduces in the same

proportion as the ratio of the eccentricity and the radius of gyration.
- The predicted results are in close agreement with the present experimental results and those of other investigators.

(Journal of Composites for Construction)

2. 选择正确的词汇填空,补全短文。

| approach | complementary | Furthermore | literature |
| Ongoing | overlooked | shortcomings | void |

The key ____1____ of extant freight models are that: (1) the theoretical justification for most models is commonly lacking; (2) the models are commonly primitive analytically; (3) there is a distinct lack of suitable data for the models; and (4) a given transport network may evolve rapidly enough that the physical transport data that do exist for freight are only useful for a few years. The ____2____ proposed in this paper addresses these issues by proposing: (1) a behaviorally rich framework within a theoretical framework of preferences, choices and constraints; (2) an econometric modeling structure and relevant stated choice data across agents for the economic situation of interest; and (3) a set of key behavioral relationships (i. e. , elasticities and agent interaction effects) that have a relatively longer "shelf life" than physical transport data.

The paucity of data on urban freight, combined with the relatively short time period for which extant urban freight data are useful, is well-known in the modeling community. ____3____, urban freight models need to be developed to exploit whatever data exist for the most robust implications that can be attained. The use of interactive SP experiments allows us to avoid the predominant data constraints through the collection of primary data that are directly tied to the model they are intended to serve.

The merit of existing methods should not be ____4____, and indeed both the current and proposed methods are ____5____. That is, transport models serve a proven and significant purpose in transport planning and policy. The introduction of a new approach for expanding the knowledge of the preferences of urban freight agents, and the process by which those preferences are manifested into urban goods movement outcomes, is an opportunity to enrich the existing models.

While much of the ____6____ on logistics chains emphasizes decisions and relationships between agents, there appears to be a ____7____ in formal methods of specification of a behavioral model, as well as a mechanism for investigating the behavioral support for specific policies that can contribute to the redefinition of the urban freight distribution task in a way that can improve the performance of the existing infrastructure. Issues such as reducing traffic congestion are increasingly high on government agendas, yet establishing the role of congestion charging regimes and their effectiveness in delivering benefits to the agents in a supply chain are poorly understood. ____8____ research using the ideas set out in this paper is designed to contribute to filling this void.

3. 将如下结论中的句子还原回正确位置。

No.	Sentences	Positions
A	but the case itself offers several lessons and suggests areas for further research and refinement	
B	However, there is hope that others might undertake field applications to help see how	
C	In addition, further work needs to be done in relation to	
D	our exercise was conducted in the confines of academia	
E	The goal of scenario planning is not to	
F	Though the analysis is admittedly rough and preliminary in scope	
G	With the goal of advancing the possibility for	

Conclusions

Scenario planning is a strategic-planning approach well-known for its ability to get decision makers to think outside of the box, and to enable organizations to make decisions in a world of increasing uncertainty and unpredictability and to produce robust strategies. ____1____ produce a more precise portrait of tomorrow, but rather more sound and robust decision today.

Scenario planning continues to be used across a range of disciplines and sectors. In metropolitan-transportation planning, although several examples exist from the 1970s and 1980s, more recent scenario-planning applications are scant in the literature. The challenges for incorporating long-term strategic vision into metropolitan-transportation planning have not, however, gone away. ____2____ scenario planning to contribute to the study and long-term planning of regional transportation system, this paper has presented the framework used in an academic application to the Houston metropolitan region.

Drawing from examples from other sectors, the scenario literature, and some precedents from the field of transportation, the Houston case adapted an eight-step scenario-planning approach. ____3____, we believe it contributes a step forward inusing scenario planning for regional strategic transportation planning framework. Not only do the steps outlined provide a logical planning framework, ____4____.

Among the points raised in our evaluation of Houston application, perhaps the most important one relates to the fact that ____5____. This inevitably limits the case's ability to shed light on how the proposed process might fit into the institutional, procedural, and political confines of real-life strategic scenario-planning process. ____6____ determining an ideal number of scenarios for transportation planning, testing the scenarios for consistency, and linking scenario planning to quantitative transportation planning and evaluation tools. The use of scenario-planning in the context of Mexico City air-quality-management project currently underway, in which the first two writers of this paper are involved, will hopefully help to answer some of these questions. ____7____ planning agencies can adapt the proposed approach and how the approach might compare in use and ultimate results with other approaches. The ultimate goal is to help regional planning authorities, the private sectors, and citizens in the development of robust transportation strategies in time of uncertainty.

4. 将下列结论中各要素所表述的内容正确连线。

（1）A detailed description of the method and experimental results can be found in a subsequent paper.

（2）The method has been extended to address the problem of bearing prognostics.

总结与回顾

讨论与评述

（3）We introduced a new bearing fault detection and diagnosis scheme based on hidden Markov modeling (HMM) of vibration signals. In this new scheme, HMM models were trained to present various bearing conditions. These models were then used to detect both single- and multiple-bearing faults based on the model probabilities. The new scheme was tested with experimental data collected from an accelerometer measuring the vibration from the drive-end ball bearing of an induction motor-driven mechanical system. It was shown that this method is very accurate in the detection and diagnosis of both single-and multiple-bearing faults under different operating conditions, i.e., load and speed.

建议与展望

4.5 相关阅读

1. Supplementary Reading Material 1
What is a Conclusion ?

Conclusion is the chronological end of any discussion. It is the stopping point of a detailed argument. Basically, its occurrence ends rest of the debate. Whether you are going through a research paper, essay or thesis, you always require strong concluding remarks to leave an impact on your readers.

Writing a good conclusion is not an easy deal. You should have a bulk of catchy words and phrases for conclusions that can make your writing more interesting for your audience. Moreover, you can also search online examples for writing your own conclusions.

Legal Definition of a Conclusion

Technically, we can define conclusion as, an end of any discussion and the point where final arguments are made. After concluding remarks, nothing new can be presented even forgotten by the writer. This is a place where final decisions or arguments are made.

Some More Definitions of a Conclusion

Here are some more definitions of a conclusion:

- **An Ending or Finishing Point**: As it has been already mentioned that conclusion is a finishing point. It sums up all the discussion within a paragraph.
- **Conclusion as an Outcome**: Conclusions can be defined as an outcome where results of an experiment, act or theory can be enclosed. So, it can be defined and taken in more technical terms.
- **Conclusions as a Judgment**: Those research papers or essays that involve discussion always require some decision or judgment at the end. So, conclusion can be defined as a portion of the paper where final decisions or judgment is made after complete discussion.
- **Arrangement of Ideas**: Ideas are also arranged and settled within the body of a conclusion.

What Do Readers Expect from a Conclusion?

If you want to know the true meaning and definition of a conclusion, then you should concentrate what your readers expect from a closing or ending paragraph. Most often readers expect some particular points from a well written conclusion. Remember your readers have continued reading several pages before reaching at your conclusion so your ending paragraph should be catchy enough.

- The ending paragraph should summarize all the basic ideas presented within an essay or a research paper.
- If you are talking about an issue then you should present personal opinion on that particular subject as concluding remarks.
- While drawing conclusions, you can also rephrase the questions.
- If you are considering an issue in your essay or research then add future implications if the situation changes or continues.

An Important Aspect of Writing a Good Conclusion

While drawing conclusions, keep in mind an important point that never add any new information in the last part of your essay. In ending paragraph, audience or readers do not expect anything new. Conclusion should have precise information. Do not repeat concepts and words that have been already mentioned. However, you should have enough synonyms and related words that can make your conclusion more attractive.

Writing a Good Conclusion

From the above mentioned definition, it is now crystal clear that the conclusion is made to indicate the end of a research or an essay. It is drawn to summarize the basic points of any discussion. So, it must be written keeping in mind the following points:

- to encourage the audience or readers;
- to intensify the points made in an essay;
- to arouse the emotions of the readers;

- to restate arguments and facts with logic;

...

Difference Between a Conclusion and a Summary

Some people confuse summary with conclusion. Be focused that both are absolutely different and diverse approaches ending an essay. Summary involves the points in precise manners that have been already mentioned within the essay body. On the other hand, conclusion can be defined as an ending paragraph that offers more interesting and clear approach. It does not simply replicate what you have already done in your essay.

So, you should be careful that your conclusion should neither be a simple restatement of your essay nor a summary. It must go beyond. It should be a judgment for your thesis or it may express your consent for an issue. Findings and implications are also discussed in a conclusion. Sometimes directives are also put forward as concluding remarks.

(http://www.writeawriting.com/academic-writing/definition-of-conclusion/)

2. Supplementary Reading Material 2

Dissertation Conclusion Structure

A solid structure for a dissertation conclusion should look like the following structure:

Conclusion (the Last Chapter)

- Introduction;
- Research Objectives: Summary of Findings and Conclusions;
- Recommendations;
- Contribution to knowledge(For Doctorate Students Only);
- Limitations;
- Self-reflection.

The introduction part of your dissertation conclusion revives the reader's memory about your research aims and objectives and gives a quick run-down on the content of your concluding section.

In the Research Objectives: Summary of Findings and Conclusions, to the subsequent questions:

- As a result of your Literature Review and empirical research (if you did both), what individual research objectives did you find out?
- What conclusions have you drawn thereby?

For each research objective, make your findings clear to the readers and offer a view on what your research is telling you.

Your dissertation conclusion is actually a derivative of your research findings and the recommendations are based on your dissertation conclusion. In Recommendation part of your dissertation conclusion, you show two types of recommendations as:

- recommendations linked to your conclusions;

- recommendations as suggestions for future research.

This part of dissertation conclusion begins with the comprehensive explanation of your recommendations with practical and rational ways or their implementations.

In general, this is not mandatory for Master's students to make a contribution to knowledge. However, if it is, you have to add a subsection in your dissertation conclusion section entitled Contribution to Knowledge. This subsection should consider your contribution in two ways:
- contribution as a result of your Literature Review findings and your empirical work;
- contribution by comparing and contrasting your work/findings against the work of other researchers.

In the Limitations, you show that your research work meets the standard in reference to the conceived practical and theoretical limitations. For example, impossibility, inability, lack of time, restrictions, etc. This is not utterly essential to make a Limitations subsection as long as you refer to the limitations of your work in between the dissertation conclusion. What you can do is to smartly turn some of the limitations into recommendations.

In the Self-reflection, reflect on two questions: "What advice would you give to other students" and "If you had to do it [your dissertation] again, what would you do differently, if anything?"

(http://www.dissertationswriting.co.uk/dissertation_conclusion.htm)

3. Supplementary Reading Material 3
Conclusion of a Report

The conclusion summarizes the major inferences that can be drawn from the information presented in the report. It answers the questions raised by the original research problem or stated purpose of the report and states the conclusions reached. Finally, the conclusion of your report should also attempt to show "what it all means": the significance of the findings reported and their impact.

The conclusion(s) presented in a report must be related to resulting from and justified by the material which appears in the report. The conclusion must not introduce any new material. It should report on all the conclusions that the evidence dictates as it is NOT the job of a conclusion to "gloss over conclusions that are puzzling, unpleasant, incomplete or don't seem to fit into your scheme". Doing this would indicate writer bias and mean your conclusion may mislead the reader.

In the workplace, conclusions are quite often read by managers before the main text of the report and hence, should summarize the main points clearly. This section also may include:
- reference to original aim(s) and objective(s) of the report;
- application(s) of results;
- limitations and advantages of the findings;

- objective opinion, evaluation or judgment of the evidence.

Quite often the present tense is used in the conclusion; for example, "The healthy lifestyles concept analyzed in this report is a good candidate for next phase of the marketing campaign for Choice chocolate".

The conclusions may be ordered in several ways. The main conclusion may be stated first and then any other conclusions in decreasing order of importance. Alternatively, it may be better to organize the conclusions in the same order as the body section was organized. Another strategy would be to present the positive conclusions together and then the negative conclusions. The organizational strategy you use may vary; the important thing is that the organization of your conclusion is logical.

The conclusion must arise from the evidence discussed in the body of the report. It should not, therefore, subjectively tell the reader what to do: This job is performed by the recommendations section.

(NOTE: sometimes the conclusion and recommendations can be presented together in one section but they should be presented in separately labeled subsections).

(http://unilearning.uow.edu.au/report/4bv.html)

4. Supplementary Reading Material 4

Tips for Writing a Strong Conclusion

Bring out the significance of your research paper. Show how you've brought closure to the research problem, and point out remaining gaps in knowledge by suggesting issues for further research. Deal with issues at the level of the whole paper rather than with issues at the level of a paragraph.

Make the significance brought out in the conclusion congruent with the argument of your paper. Don't oversell or undersell the significance of your paper. The conclusion can't reach any farther than the paper's main argument. The conclusion is the place to put the final, proper perspective on the paper as a whole.

Bring closure to the entire paper, not only by summarizing the arguments, but also by bringing out the significance of the paper. Avoid using terms related to specific elements of the paper—look at the paper as a whole and pull it all together in the conclusion. Take the thesis statement from your introduction and demonstrate in your conclusion how the paper as a whole has addressed the research problem.

Make the conclusion sell a worthwhile paper to the interested readers. Exercise integrity in your conclusion—don't exaggerate the conclusion to bring strength to a weak paper. There should be a strong correlation between the arguments in your paper and your stated significance(s) in the conclusion. In the case of a thesis or dissertation, readers will likely turn first to the conclusion. Don't let your readers get motivated by your conclusion to read the rest of the document—only to experience disappointment.

Use key terms, concepts and phrases from the introduction and body of the paper—but don't just repeat them. Use them to bring out the new insight gained from your research. The conclusion should provide more than a flat-footed restatement of the thesis statement articulated in the introduction—it should take the entire paper a step ahead toward a new level of insight on the research problem.

Make the tone of the conclusion match the tone of the rest of the paper. For most of your papers, keep the tone serious—omit jokes and anecdotes from the conclusion. In the context of an academic argument, humor is generally inappropriate and could seriously detract from your paper's credibility.

Write the conclusion at a level of specificity/generality that matches the introduction. Don't use the conclusion to summarize the previous paragraph—rather, pull the entire paper together and make its significance clear. For a book, deal with the primary issues raised in the introduction and in each of the chapters. A concluding chapter should draw conclusions for each major issues raised in the document. For any type of paper, don't overreach the conclusion—make statements that can be fully supported by your evidence. The body of the paper should prime readers for the conclusion—if the conclusion surprises them, readers may distrust the reasoning of the entire paper.

In a thesis or dissertation, it's usually customary to raise questions or suggest areas for further research. If this is done in a 20-page research paper, it's normally only a sentence or two—not even a paragraph. At this point, the writer must keep moving toward closure.

Don't introduce any new information into the conclusion. The conclusion signals readers that the writer will point out the significance of the paper at this point, and bring the entire paper to a clear and definite end. Just as the minister should never introduce a new point in the concluding remarks of a sermon, the writer should not introduce another point in the conclusion. Expecting the end, readers will be disappointed—or annoyed—to find yet more new information.

Put your best writing skills into the conclusion, especially if you are writing a thesis or dissertation. Never allow the first draft to stand as the final product—revise the conclusion again and again until its integrity is practically unassailable. Scholars frequently read the conclusion of a thesis, dissertation or research article first!

When writing a 20-page paper, limit the conclusion to one full paragraph. You might take two or three paragraphs to narrow down to the finish line, but you should pack the final punch into only one paragraph. One well-written paragraph can deliver far more rhetorical "punch" than a three-paragraph peroration.

(http://acc. roberts. edu/nemployees/hamilton _ barry/tips%20for%20writing%20a%20strong%20conclusion. htm)

第5章 致谢

5.1 概述

作为英文学术论文不可或缺的一部分,致谢是以简短的文字对课题研究或论文撰写过程中直接或间接给予帮助的人员或机构(如指导教师、同事、同学、相关赞助机构等)表达诚挚的谢意,这不仅是一种礼貌,也是对他人劳动的尊重,是治学者应有的基本素养。

5.2 构成要素

英文学术论文的致谢包含五个部分:资金支持/赞助,表达感谢,免责陈述,论文其他版本,来源。由于研究性质、内容、过程等方面的差异,在五个构成要素中,只有"表达感谢"是必需性要素,研究者须根据当前研究的性质和特点对其他要素做出选择。

1. 资金支持/赞助

资金支持/赞助即描述当前研究的资金来源等相关信息。资金来源可能是个人,也可能是机构。需要注意的是,如果研究项目由多方支持,必须明确并逐一说明。项目号通常放在赞助方之前。

参见下例:

例 1 **This research was supported by Grant** BFF2002-01315 from Ministerio de Ciencia y Tecnología and **by Grant** SA062/02 from Junta de Castilla y León (Spain).

本研究是在……和……的资金支持下完成的,项目号分别为……和……。

例 2 **This work was partially supported by** Spanish Ministry of Education and Science through the Logic Tools project TIN2004-03382(all authors), the FPU **grant** AP2002-3533 (Oliveras) and National Science Foundation (NSF) **grant** 0237422 (Tinelli and Oliveras).

本研究是在……以及……的部分资金支持下完成的。

2. 表达感谢

表达感谢即学术论文致谢的核心内容,对给予研究工作直接和间接支持的人员或机构表达诚挚的谢意。感谢的对象可以是指导教师、审稿人、同事、同学、被试、相关赞助机构等。

参见下例:

例 1 **The author is grateful to** Janos Simon and Josh Grochow for helpful discussions, and to the referees for helpful comments.

作者对……表示感谢。

例2　**The author would like to thank** Prof. Tatsuya Akutsu for fruitful discussions on protein comparison algorithms.

作者感谢……

3. 免责陈述

免责指作者当前研究中的观点不代表资助机构或资助人的立场。

参见下例：

例1　However，**the opinions expressed here do not necessarily reflect the policy** of the National Science Foundation.

此处观点不代表……的政策。

例2　**None，however，is responsible for any remaining errors.**

除本人外，其他人员和机构对文中存在的错误不负责任。

4. 论文其他版本

论文其他版本即论文在正式发表之前，曾经以某种形式在相关学术场合进行过交流，如学术研讨、学术会议等。

参见下例：

例1　**Preliminary versions of this article appeared in** Electronic **Colloquium** on Computational Complexity (ECCC). Tech. Rep. TR06-127，2006 and in Proceedings of the 39th ACM **Symposium** on Theory of Computing (STOC)，ACM，New York，2007，pp. 266-274.

本文初期版本曾在……研讨会上进行过交流，并收入……会议论文集。

例2　**An earlier version of this paper was presented at** the UN Climate Summit.

本论文早前版本曾在……做过发言。

5. 来源

来源即须说明研究成果是否是基于博士学位论文的研究。

参见下例：

例1　**This paper is based on** the research completed as partial fulfillment for **the Ph. D. requirements** at the University of Sheffield.

本文是基于……博士学位论文进行的研究。

需要注意的是，致谢中通常使用第一人称。一位作者用"I"，有多个作者则用"We"。也可以使用如"the present authors"来表达，但是这种表达方式过于正式。以上各要素中，通常先说明"资金支持/赞助"，然后"表达感谢"；而"免责陈述"可以根据研究的具体情况选择性使用。如果需要描述"论文其他版本"和"来源"，则可以放在"致谢"的起始或结尾。此外，如果是学位论文，"表达感谢"应该放在"致谢"的起始位置。

5.3　写作范式

英文学术论文的致谢因研究性质、内容等方面的不同，在撰写过程中会呈现出一定差异。但是，学术论文致谢写作存在规律性，是有一定的写作范式可以遵循的。

1. 资金支持/赞助的写作范式

介绍资金支持/赞助时，常用到的表达范式如表 5-1 所示。

表 5-1　资金支持/赞助的写作范式

The work was supported by …	本研究由……提供资金支持
The study was partially supported by …	本研究由……提供部分资金支持
Support for this work was provided by …	本研究资金支持由……提供
This research was partially supported by a grant … from …	本研究由……提供部分资金支持，项目号为……
This research was funded by Contract … from …	本研究由……资助，项目号为……

参见下例：

例 1　**This work is a key project funded by** the State Education Commission and **is also supported by** the National Social Sciences Foundation.

本研究是受……和……资助的重点项目。

例 2　**This work is supported in part by** the Defense Advanced Research Projects Agency under Contract No. 0039-94-c-0165 and **in part by** the Hewlett-Packard Company under its AI University Grants Program.

本研究所用资金分别来自……和……，项目号为……

2. 表达感谢的写作范式

表达感谢是致谢的核心部分，是一个必需性要素，常用的写作范式如表 5-2 所示。

表 5-2　表达感谢的写作范式

We are grateful to … The authors wish to thank … for … We would like to thank … for … I want to thank … I want to extend my acknowledgement to … I am/We are indebted to … I wish to express my gratitude to … My thanks go to … Thanks are due to … Thanks are extended to …	谨向……表达感谢

参见下例：

例 1　**The author wishes to thank** the following of the Burnaby School District, British Columbia, Canada, for their contribution to this research project：Ms. S. Pierce（Principal），Ms. M. Elgaard, Ms. J. Duhamel Conover, Ms. L. Meltzer, Ms. S. DeSivia, Ms. L. Wilson, Mr. A. Wong, Ms. A. Businskas and all the students who participated in the project。

本研究的作者向……表示感谢。

例 2　**We are grateful to** Luca Trevisan for collaboration **at an early stage of** this research. **We also thank** Dan Boneh, Ran Canetti, Manoj Prabhakaran, Michael Rabin,

Emanuele Viola, Yacov Yacobi, and the anonymous reviewers of CRYPTO'01 and JACM for helpful discussions and comments.

非常感谢……给予研究初期的帮助。同时,向……表示感谢。

例3 **We are very grateful to three anonymous reviewers** for their excellent **comments and suggestions**.

对三位匿名审稿人的……意见深表感谢。

例4 **I wish to thank** my dear supervisor for his encouragement and guidance throughout this project.

向……表示感谢。

例5 **The authors wish to thank** David Beglar, Paul Meara, Paul Nation, and Gladys Valcourt for insightful comments on earlier drafts of this paper.

作者感谢……

例6 **We would like to thank** Roberto Sebastiani for a number of insightful discussions and comments on the lazy SMT approach and DPLL(T). **We are also grateful to** the anonymous referees for their helpful suggestions on improving this article.

我们感谢……。同时,感谢……

例7 **I am indebted to** Madhu Sudan for expressing his optimism regarding viability of the approach taken in this paper at an early stage of the work. **I would also like to thank** him for many helpful in-depth technical discussions. **Many thanks to** Oded Goldreich, Nick Harvey, Kiran Kedlaya, Swastik Kopparty, Dieter van Melkebeek and David Woodruff for **their valuable comments**.

对……感激不已,也要感谢……。同时,向……提出的宝贵意见表示感谢。

例8 **I am grateful to** the two anonymous ESP Journal reviewers and Brian Paltridge for their detailed and insightful comments **on an earlier version of this paper. My deep thanks also go to** Fred Davidson and Sara Cushing Weigle **for their moral support**.

非常感谢……对论文初稿提出的意见。对……给予的精神上的支持表达真挚的谢意。

例9 **The author would like to thank** Prof. Tatsuya Akutsu for fruitful discussions on protein comparison algorithms. **All the computational experiments in this research were done** on the Super Computer System, Human Genome Center, Institute of Medical Science, University of Tokyo.

作者感谢……,所有的计算实验都是在……完成的。

例10 **My thanks go to** my colleague James Houle, and to the two anonymous reviewers for their valuable feedback on earlier versions of this paper.

感谢……

例11 **We would like to express our indebtedness** to the reviewer, whose searching questions helped us elaborate and improve our argument.

向……表达我们的谢意。

例12 **I appreciate the help of** John Rivlin who granted permission to reprint the two figures in the paper.

感谢……的帮助。

3. 免责陈述的写作范式（见表 5-3）

表 5-3　免责陈述的写作范式

However, the opinions expressed here do not necessarily reflect the policy of …	此处观点不代表……的政策
The interpretations in this paper remain my own	本文观点仅代表个人立场
None, however, is responsible for any remaining errors	本人对存在的错误负全责
However, any mistakes that remain are my own	任何错误由个人承担

参见下例：

例 1　This paper was partially financed by FONDECYT grant No. 1990338 and **reflects the views of the authors and not those of the institutions of their affiliations**.

本文观点仅代表个人立场，不代表相关机构的立场。

例 2　**The usual disclaimer applies**.

免责声明同样适用于本文。

4. 论文其他版本的写作范式（见表 5-4）

表 5-4　论文其他版本的写作范式

A preliminary version appeared in/at …	本论文的先期版本登载于……
An earlier version was presented at …	本文早期版本曾在……上做过发言

参见下例：

例 1　**The findings discussed here were first presented at** the Guilin ELT International Conference, Guilin, People's Republic of China, 19-24 July, 1993.

本论文早期版本曾在……做过发言。

例 2　**A preliminary version of this article appeared in** *Advances in Cryptology—CRYPTO'01*, Lecture Notes in Computer Science, vol. 2139, Springer-Verlag, 1-18.

本论文的早期版本曾登载于……

5. 论文来源的写作范式（见表 5-5）

表 5-5　来源的写作范式

The paper is based on the research completed as partial fulfillment for the Ph. D. requirements … The article is based on the author's doctoral dissertation …	本文是基于……博士学位论文的研究进行的

参见下例：

例 1　**This article is based on my doctoral research** with slightly different analyses.

本文是基于……博士学位论文的研究进行的。

6. 范文分析

1）范文一

S1：I thank Alister Cumming, Kumiko Inutsuka, Philip M. McCarthy, Wataru Suzuki, and Journal of Second Language Writing's anonymous reviewers for their insightful comments on earlier drafts of this article. —— 表达感谢

S2：This article is based on my doctoral research with slightly different analyses. —— 来源

(*Journal of Second Language Writing*)

2）范文二

S1：We thank Hamid Beladi and two anonymous referees for their helpful comments on a previous version of this article. —— 表达感谢

S2：We acknowledge financial support from the Faculty Research Grant program at Utah State University and from the Utah Agricultural Experiment Station, Utah State University, Logan, UT 84322-4810, by way of grant UTA 024. —— 资金支持/赞助

S3：The usual disclaimer applies. —— 免责陈述

(*International Review of Economics and Finance*)

3）范文三

S1：The work described in this article was substantially supported by grants from the Research Grants Council of the Hong Kong Special Administrative Region (Project No. B-Q714). —— 资金支持/赞助

S2：I am deeply indebted to Prof. Winnie Cheng and Prof. Martin Warren for their generous permission to let me use the *Hong Kong Corpus of Spoken English* prior to its completion and publication.

S3：I would like to thank the editor and the anonymous reviewer who provided helpful and constructive suggestions on an earlier version of this article. —— 表达感谢

S4：Any errors that remain are mine. —— 免责陈述

(*Discourse Studies*)

4）范文四

S1：I thank Dr. P. Vallejos Llobet from the Departamento de Humanidades, Universidad Nacional del Sur (UNS), for her comments, cooperation, and guidance in the present report.

S2：I am also grateful to Ms. Adriana Grossi Treadway from Arkansas University for her assistance in editing this manuscript. —— 表达感谢

S3：This work was supported by Grant 24/I126 from the Universidad Nacional del Sur (UNS) to Dr. P. Vallejos-Llobet, director of the project "Textual aspects of scientific knowledge", within which this study was carried out.

资金支持/赞助

(*English for Specific Purposes*)

5）范文五

S1：We thank Jaime Guajardo and Pamela Mellado for helping us put together the database used in this research, and Mohsin Khan and Reza Vaez-Zadeh for their valuable comments.

表达感谢

S2：This paper was partially financed by FONDECYT grant No. 1990338 and reflects the views of the authors and not those of the institutions of their affiliations.

资金支持和免责陈述

(*International Review of Financial Analysis*)

5.4 练习题

1. 英文学术论文致谢包含哪些构成要素？
2. 按照致谢的结构要素分析以下两篇致谢。

I

This work has been supported in part by the US army Armaments Research and Development Engineering Center (ARDEC) at Picatinny Arsenal, contract DAAE30-00-D1011. The author would like to express his gratitude for the ideas of Paul Kolodzy and Dan Duchamp, as well as the prototype work accomplished by Lucas Vickers, Adity Kedia, and Deepika Saluja. The author also would like to thank the anonymous reviewers for their suggestions.

II

We would like to thank the editor in chief, the area editor, and the reviewers for their helpful comments. Our thanks are also due to the ActivityFlow implementation team, especially to Roger Barga and Tong Zhou for their implementation endeavor on various components that form the basis for the ActivityFlow project and to Jesal Pandya and Iffath Zofishan for their implementation effort on the ActivityFlow specification language and its graphical user interface. This project was supported partially by an NSF CCR grant, a DARPAITO grant, and a DOE SciDAC grant.

3. 对如下两篇致谢的人称、时态、语态作简要分析。

I

This work was supported in part by the US National Science Foundation under Grant Nos. 0208567 and 0312966. The authors would like to thank Metha Jeeradit for his contributions to VPC1 and the anonymous reviewers for their helpful feedback.

II

The writers express their thanks to all who participated in this survey for their cooperation and objectivity. Additionally, the writers thank ASCE for funding this study, for providing meeting facilities, and for developing and administering the electronic version of the survey. The opinions expressed in this paper are the writers' and do not necessarily reflect the views of ASCE or the institutions with which the writers are affiliated. The writers also thank the Executive Committee of the Technical Council on Computing and Information Technology which has had the foresight to support all three of this committee's survey efforts.

4. 请将以下句子翻译成汉语。

(1) The authors acknowledge the kind assistance of Mrs. Susan Chaisson and Mrs. Loraine Maxwell in transcription, and John Griffith, Ph. D. , for biostatistics.

(2) The authors express their gratitude to Juan Lechago, MD, Department of Pathology, Baylor College of Medicine, for performing selected immunostains, and to Shelley Des Jardines and Allison Garrett of manuscript preparation.

(3) The assistance of the nursing and technical staff of the SUNY HSC Clinical Research Unit and of Suzanne Brennan is gratefully acknowledged. My thanks are also due to Ms. Sally Hodgson for secretarial contributions.

(4) We would like to thank Dr. David Robertson for his helpful suggestions in the preparation of this manuscript.

(5) Gratitude is expressed to the President of the Aga Khan University. Thanks also go to Dr. Dur and his colleagues in the School of Nursing to participate in the program, and to the students and other people who contributed to its success.

(6) This work was supported in part by the Grants-in-aid for Cancer Research (10-2) from the Ministry of Health and Welfare.

5. 请将以下句子翻译成英语。

(1) 本文的图片由××先生提供,在此表示谢意。

(2) 本课题为国家自然科学基金资助项目(××××××)。

(3) 对本研究作出贡献的其他研究人员有:××博士,××硕士。

(4) 本研究得到国际货币基金组织的资助。

5.5 相关阅读

1. Supplementary Reading Material 1

How to Write an Acknowledgement

If you were assisted in your research or in composing the paper, it would be courteous for you to express thanks, at the end of your paper in the section of "Acknowledgements", to those who helped you.

The following individuals and organizations should be acknowledged:

- Individuals who provided technical help or worthwhile advice, or even some small favor such as typing the manuscript or drawing a figure.
- Foundations or other organizations from which you obtained financial assistance, such as grants, contracts, or fellowships.
- Known or anonymous reviewers who reviewed your paper for publication or for presentation at a conference.
- Copyright holders who granted permission to use parts of a book or a paper in your work, or to produce the paper in other books or magazines either in the original language or in other languages.

(http://wenku.baidu.com/link?url=GAJrQSfz2W9z6Hk6-DKQR3FpARpCiWZskzKmrAuoXZrZNJX-Z3I5ta_Mb6byQybLl1nZ_fsV7aiBh5sjM8gDwzVoM87DYkeBuSCiF5O4YAu)

2. Supplementary Reading Material 2

How Should I Write My Paper Acknowledgements?

Writing a thesis or dissertation can be a daunting task that can take many hours, days and even years to achieve. A work of nonfiction can take even longer, as can a fictitious piece. One task you must think about as you near your paper's completion is who to thank for their help in completing the work and how they should be thanked.

Cultural Differences

Although it is a somewhat elusive and subjective thing to say, it is certainly true that nations and cultures that share a common language have some different styles in how they express themselves. Whilst discretion suggests that it is better not to be specific, some find expressions in flowing and effusive words, for example "wonderful," "stupendous," "my heart goes out" and even "great and illustrious". Other cultures are more reserved and prefer words such as "gratitude," "thanks" and "appreciation". So, especially if you are studying abroad, you should keep these points in mind when writing an acknowledgement.

Supervisor

Your supervisor will expect acknowledgements. If he/she gave you the most help, which should be the case, he/she should be the first to be named and should receive the warmest praise. Remember that he/she may continue to be of assistance in the future, either as a referee or even as a fellow academic or peer. If you do not appropriately acknowledge him/her, he/she will probably not mention it, but he/she may be offended. If you feel that your supervisor did not really help you and that your achievement was despite, rather than because of, his/her help, you should still make some acknowledgements, even if somewhat caustic or curt.

Other People Who Gave Assistance

Although there is some implicit obligation to acknowledge your supervisor, there is no such onus for others. For this reason, you should consider carefully who gave you assistance, the manner in which it was given and how much you benefitted from it. Then compile a list in the order that you see the relative help given. Remember that others will know how much help they have given and will probably have some ideas about relativity, so make sure that you are fair and objective. Academics are more sensitive than you might think.

Unwarranted Acknowledgement

Sometimes people have a way of making you feel that you should say that they have helped you when deep down you know that they haven't. Their advice may have been unhelpful and self-seeking. If you experience this, you should not give them any unwarranted acknowledgement.

Relatives and Friends

Sometimes, students feel that they should thank their parents regardless of whether they have assisted or not. This is a personal choice and nobody could question such an emotive decision. However, some acknowledgements are just too long and tedious and thank such a wide variety of people that a temptation is to ask the student if there is anybody that he/she has ever known that he has not thanked.

Words and Phrases

In the same sense, remember not to use too many words and phrases about the person that you are acknowledging. Either just acknowledge his/her help or find a summary word or phrase that states how he/she assisted you. For example, "Many thanks to my supervisor, without whose patience and wisdom this thesis could not have been completed."

(http://www.ehow.com/info_12079604_should-write-paper-acknowledgements.html)

3. Supplementary Reading Material 3

Sample 1 (Research Article Acknowledgements)

A preliminary version of this article appeared in *Advances in Cryptology—CRYPTO'01*, Lecture Notes in Computer Science, vol. 2139, Springer-Verlag, 1-18. Most of this work was done when B. Barak was a graduate student at Weizmann Institute of Science, A. Sahai was a graduate student at MIT (supported by a DOD/NDSEG Graduate Fellowship), S. Vadhan was a graduate student and a postdoctoral fellow at MIT (supported by a DOD/NDSEG Graduate Fellowship and an NSF Mathematical Sciences Postdoctoral Research Fellowship), and K. Yang was a graduate student at CMU. Further support for this work was provided to B. Barak by NSF grants 0627526 and 0426582, US-Israel BSF grant 2004288, and Packard and Sloan fellowships; to O. Goldreich by the Minerva Foundation (Germany) and the Israel Science Foundation (Grant No. 460/05); to A. Sahai by a Sloan Research Fellowship, an Okawa Research Award, and NSF grants 0205594, 0312809, 0456717, 0627781, 0716389, 0830803, 0916574, 1065276, 1118096, and 1136174; and to S. Vadhan by NSF grants 0430336 and 0831289, a Guggenheim Fellowship, and the Miller Institute for Basic Research in Science.

Sample 2 (Research Article Acknowledgements)

The writers gratefully acknowledge the partial support of this research by the National Science Foundation under Grant Nos. CMS 95-00301 and CMS 95-28083 (Dr. S. C. Liu, Program Director) and the Central Research Institute of Electric Power Industry in Japan. The writers would also like to acknowledge the generous efforts of Professor Erik A. Johnson, Univ. of Southern California Department of Civil and Environmental Engineering, in editing and providing detailed comments on this paper and the corresponding MATLAB programs.

Sample 3 (Research Article Acknowledgements)

We would like to express our thanks to H. P. Lu of Tsinghua University and T. Miyagi of Gifu University for their valuable discussions. We are also grateful to the anonymous referees and M. G. H. Bell of Imperial College London for their comments that have improved the presentation of the paper and stimulated a few important issues for further research as well. The second author acknowledges the financial support by a grant from the Research Grants Council of the Hong Kong Special Administrative Region, China (Project No. HKUST6033/02E).

Sample 4 (Thesis/Dissertation Acknowledgements)

My deepest gratitude goes first and foremost to Professor ×××, my supervisor, for her constant encouragement and guidance. She has walked me through all the stages of the writing of this thesis. Without her consistent and illuminating instruction, this thesis could not have reached its present form.

Second, I would like to express my heartfelt gratitude to Professor ×××, who led me into the world of translation. I am also greatly indebted to the professors and teachers at the Department of English: Professor ×××, Professor ×××, who have instructed and helped me a lot in the past two years.

Last, my thanks would go to my beloved family for their loving considerations and great confidence in me all through these years. I also owe my sincere gratitude to my friends and my fellow classmates who gave me their help and time in listening to me and helping me work out my problems during the difficult course of the thesis.

Sample 5 (Thesis/Dissertation Acknowledgements)

The accomplishment of this paper benefits from the enlightenment of my supervisor, associate Professor, ×××, whose inspiring insights, generous encouragements, and enthusiastic instructions have facilitated me much throughout my thesis writing. Her penetrating and insightful comments provide me with inspiring source. She has been in constant concern about my paper, spared no pains to read my thesis draft. I would also like to extend my sincere thanks to the Foreign Language Department of Fuyang University as well as all my teachers. Thanks to their instructive guidance and comprehensive education during the four years' schooling, I can acquire the opportunity to further my study in English. Finally, my great gratitude also goes to those writers and editors whose works I have benefited greatly from without which the completion of the thesis would not have been possible.

Sample 6 (Thesis/Dissertation Acknowledgements)

Writing a thesis is done by a single person: the one who graduates. However, doing research and gaining knowledge can not be done without the help of other people. Writing a protocol, aimed to be an international standard, is, despite that it probably will be published as an "experimental" instead of a "standard" protocol, is not an effort I would attempt on my own. It is sometimes hard to discriminate between the work I did on my own and the work done by others. I have written the chapter about PAP, CHAP and EAP (called "Supporting various client Authentication Protocols"), but I lost count on the number of times others authors rewrote it. Likewise, I hope some of my input improved the other chapters.

Co-authors

My gratitude goes to all co-authors. In particular I would like to thank John Vollbrecht for his endless questions and patient answers. He did make me feel comfortable, in particular when I presented some slides at the IETF conference for a room full of people. My thanks also go to Walter Weiss, who pushed the drafts and got everybody writing. He astounded me twice by compiling the draft at the last minutes before the deadline, even though that seemed impossible to me. I still wonder how he managed it—even if he didn't sleep! A special thank goes to Ravi Sahita who kindly took the time in Salt Lake City to sit down and explain some details about the accessor issues which must have been obvious, but I completely misunderstood. Gratitude to Kwok Ho Chan, who showed in Minneapolis that he is a good technician and lobbyist, and is nice to talk to. A last thanks goes to Dave Durham, who showed, when I feared disaster when I had to give a talk to the RAP group, there was nothing to fear about. In the mean time he elevated my knowledge about what I was doing. I am indebted to Cees de Laat, who supervised me, and kept an eye on what I was doing, even though he moved from Utrecht University to University of Amsterdam during work. In particular I am very grateful for the way he allowed me to work on my own pace, but still took the decision to get me on track when I got stuck in the original 802.1x work. Also, he was very generous by sponsoring my attendance at two IETF-conferences, held in the USA and reserving money from his research budget to cover my expenses there.

Family and friends

A hug and thanks go to my parents, Hennie and Wil Dijkstra, who showed me that they have faith in me, despite the fact it took me a long time to get to the point where I am now. I would like to thank everybody who pre-reviewed my thesis and gave valuable feedback, particularly my dad, for catching logical errors and to Floris de Vooys, for keeping overview. Love and kisses to Caroline Mattheij, for all the typos she caught. Additional thanks to John Vollbrecht, Leon Gommans, David van de Vliet and Reinoud Koornstra for their comments. Last, thanks to all others: Richard, Frank, Nils, Thijs, Jeroen, Arjan, Guus, René and Thomas.

My computer

Despite that I'm a Macintosh "Freak", hardly any thanks goes to the applications on my Mac, by crashing as much as 271 times since I started to write my thesis (101 days). Only thanks to MacsBugs I didn't loose count. (Least stable apps: Internet Explorer: 82 crashes; MS Word: 34 crashes; Opera: 5-21 crashes. Most stable apps: Nifty Telnet, BBEdit and DragThing, which I used just as often but "only" crashed respectively 2, 2 and 3 times).

Sample 7 (Monograph Acknowledgements)

A number of people helped this book on its way. My grateful thanks in particular to Sonia Critchley, Dick Hudson, Ann Jefferies, Alison Love, Barbara Mardell, Andrew Morrison, Chana Moshenska and Jeremy Nicholls. Earlier versions of the book were tried out with students on the MA in Applied English Linguistics at the University of Zimbabwe in 1993 and on the first year of the BA Applied Language at the University of Brighton in 1994. Their responses led to many improvements. None of these people is responsible for any remaining shortcomings. Thanks also to Julia Hall, Alison Foyle and Emma Cotter at Routledge for their commitment and hard work.

Sample 8 (Monograph Acknowledgements)

My principal acknowledgement for any knowledge I have about intonation must be to my teachers Gordon Arnold and Doc O'Connor; the influence of their teaching and of their book pervades large chunks of this book. If the study of intonation is now developing a body of theoretical discussion, this is only happening because of the existence of prior and thorough basic descriptions, and of these O'Connor and Arnold's *Intonation of Colloquial English* is pre-eminent. It should also be apparent that the two recent writers on the theory of intonation who have influenced me most are Bod Ladd and Carios Gussenhoven; while in the area of universals, the chief influence has been that of Dwight Bolinger. I must also acknowledge a debt to various colleagues with whom I have discussed intonation over many years and who have provided me with many examples: David Allerton, Edward Carney, Alan Cruse, Martin French, and John Payne. Postgraduate students have also supplied me with examples: in particular I mention Mangat Bhardwaj, Madalena Cruz-Ferreira, Eric Jarman, and Graham Low. My thanks to John Trim, who has provided helpful criticism of the whole manuscript; to David Faber, who has critically dissected almost every sentence both for content and for style, besides being the most fertile of all sources of examples; and to Penny Carter, who has always been a most helpful in-house editor. And my final thanks go to those who provided the secretarial assistance, principally Eunice Baker, and, to a lesser extent, Patricia Bowden and Irene Pickford.

Sample 9 (Monograph Acknowledgements)

The creation of these materials stemmed from the need to help international students develop the study skills necessary to function effectively on academic courses in a university context. The rationale behind the material is that students need to develop the confidence and competence to become autonomous learners in order to successfully carry out research and complete assignments, such as extended pieces of written work or oral presentations.

The development of these materials has been a collaborative effort which goes far beyond the collaboration between the authors. The material has evolved over several years of pre-sessional teaching at the Centre for Applied Language Studies at the University of Reading. There have been significant additions from a number of teachers, who have either contributed ideas or given extensive feedback on the materials. The number of teachers involved is too large for us to mention each one individually, but they are all fully appreciated.

In something like their present form, the materials have been trailed on successive pre-sessional courses at the University of Reading since 2001. This trailing has involved almost a thousand students, and they too have provided feedback in terms of course evaluation, as well as with their response to the tasks in the programme. We very much appreciate the contribution of students whose work has been adapted and incorporated into the materials.

We would particularly like to thank Jill Riley for her meticulous editing and typing up of the materials and Corinne Boz and Bruce Howell for their very significant contributions to the development of the accompanying on-line tasks.

附录A 文字指南

1. 衔接语

衔接语的恰当使用可以使语义更为清晰，给读者传递明确的信息，如举例、对比、转折、因果、给出结论等。以下是英文学术论文写作过程中部分常用的衔接语。

1) 表示"增加(addition)"的衔接语

moreover, and, in addition, again, also, as well as, furthermore, what's more,…

例1　I am majoring in architecture; **furthermore**, I spent three years in engineering.

2) 表示"方位(place)"的衔接语

beyond, to the left/rigit, over, be adjacent to, be opposite to, next to, beneath, where, inside,…

例2　Here is the switch that turns on the corridor lights. **To the right** is the switch that dims them.

3) 表示"时间(time)"的衔接语

first, next, second, then, meanwhile, at length, later, now, the next day, in the meantime, in turn, subsequently, while, since, before, after, afterward,…

例3　The crew will arrange the tables in the hall in this morning; immediately **afterward** we will do the decorations.

4) 表示"对比(comparison)"的衔接语

likewise, in the same way, in comparison, similarly,…

例4　Our reservoir is drying up because of the drought; **similarly**, water supplies in neighboring towns are dangerously low.

5) 表示"对照/转折(contrast)"的衔接语

however, but, nevertheless, on the other hand, yet, on the contrary, still, although, notwithstanding, in contrast, conversely, otherwise,…

例5　**Although** Jack worked hard, he was never promoted.

6) 表示"结果(result)"的衔接语

thus, hence, therefore, because, consequently, thereupon, as a result, so, as a consequence, accordingly,…

例6　He fooled around; **consequently**, he was shot by a furious man.

7) 表示"举例(example)"的衔接语

for example, for instance, to illustrate, namely, specifically,…

例 7 The competition for jobs is fierce; **for example**, 200 students applied for the manager's job.

8) 表示"解释(explanation)"的衔接语

that is, in other words, in fact, simply state, put another way, as a matter of fact, in effect,…

例 8 She had a terrible semester; **that is**, she failed in all the examinations.

9) 表示"总结/结论(summary or conclusion)"的衔接语

in short, in a word, in brief, to conclude, to sum up, in conclusion, in summary, all in all, to summarize, in closing, on the whole, generally, in retrospect,…

例 9 Our credit is destroyed, our bank account is overdrawn, and our debts are piling up; **in short**, we are bankrupt.

2. 易误用或易混淆词汇

accept: to receive, to give an affirmation answer
except: to exclude, to omit, to leave out

advice: counsel, recommendation (noun)
advise: to suggest to, to recommend (verb)

affect: to influence, to alter (verb)
effect: to bring about (verb)
effect: result or consequence (noun)

all ready: prepared
already: previously

all right: completely right
alright: OK—considered by some as incorrect usage of "all right"

altogether: completely or thoroughly
all together: in unison, in a group

among: refers to three or more
between: refers to two only

amount: quantity (of uncountable material)
number: a total of countable units

anyone: any person in general
any one: a specific person or item

complement: that which completes or supplements
compliment: flattery or praise, expression of regard

confidant: person in whom one confides (noun)
confident: positive or sure (adjective)

continual: taking place in close succession, frequently repeated
continuous: without stopping, without a break

credible: believable or acceptable
creditable: praiseworthy
credulous: gullible

currant: fruit
current: belonging to present time, motion of air or water

dependent: depending, relying (adjective)
dependant: one who depends on another for support (noun)

discreet: prudent, circumspect
discrete: separate entity, individual

disinterested: neutral, not biased
uninterested: not concerned with, lacking interest

disorganized: disordered
unorganized: not organized and planned

eminent: outstanding, prominent
imminent: very near, impending, threatening

farther: refers to geographical or linear distance
further: more, in addition to

forgo: abstain from, go without
forego: precede, go before

formally: according to convention
formerly: previously

imply: to hint at, or to allude to in speaking or writing
infer: to draw a conclusion from what has been said or written

its: a possessive singular pronoun
it's: a contraction for "it is"

less: smaller quantity of uncountable material
fewer: a smaller total of countable units

maybe: perhaps (adverb)
may be: indicated possibility (verb)

moral: a principle, maxim, or lesson (noun); ethical (adjective)
morale: a state of mind or psychological outlook (noun)

oral: by word of mouth
verbal: in words whether oral or written

personal: private, not public or general
personnel: the staff of an organization

practical: not theoretical, useful, pragmatic
practicable: can be put into practice (should not be used to refer to people)

proceed: to begin, to move, to advance
precede: to go before

principal: of primary importance (adjective), head of a college, chief (noun)
principle: a fundamental truth (noun)

stationery: writing paper or writing materials
stationary: not moving, fixed

3. 易拼写错误词汇表

A

正确拼写	错误拼写	正确拼写	错误拼写
absence	absense	accommodate	accommodate
academic	acedemic	achieve	acheive
access	acces	acknowledge	aknowledge
accessible	accessible	acquainted	aquainted

续表

正确拼写	错误拼写	正确拼写	错误拼写
adequate	adequite	appropriate	approprite
advertisement	advertisment	arguable	argueable
agreeable	agreable	arrangement	arrangment
among	amon	ascertain	acertain
appearance	appearence	ascend	asend

B

正确拼写	错误拼写	正确拼写	错误拼写
beautiful	beutiful	benefit	benifit
behaviour/behavior	behevior	benign	benighn
beginning	begining	brevity	brievity
believe	beleive	business	busness

C

正确拼写	错误拼写	正确拼写	错误拼写
calculate	caculate	competent	compitent
certain	certin	competitive	compititive
challenge	chanllege	conceal	conceel
circumstance	circumstence	conceive	concieve
changeable	changable	conscientious	conscientous
choice	chioce	conscious	consious
colleague	colleag	controversy	controvercy
committee	comittee	correspondence	corespondence
commitment	committment	create	creat
comparative	comperative	criticism	critisism

D

正确拼写	错误拼写	正确拼写	错误拼写
damage	damege	dependent	dependant
decision	desision	disappointed	disapointed
deficiency	defeciency	discipline	disipline
definite	defenite	disappear	dispear

E

正确拼写	错误拼写	正确拼写	错误拼写
eighth	eigth	essential	esential
efficiency	effeciency	excellent	excelent
embarrassed	embarassed	excitement	excitment
emergency	emurgency	exercise	exrcise
eminent	emenent	expense	expence
environment	enviroment	extremely	extremly

F

正确拼写	错误拼写	正确拼写	错误拼写
faithfully	faithfuly	forty	fourty
familiar	familar	friend	freind
February	Februery	fulfill	fufill
financial	finacial	fundamental	fundemental

G

正确拼写	错误拼写	正确拼写	错误拼写
gauge	guauge	guard	gard
government	goverment	guarantee	garantee

H

正确拼写	错误拼写	正确拼写	错误拼写
height	hight	hypothesis	hypothisis

I

正确拼写	错误拼写	正确拼写	错误拼写
illustrate	ilustrate	inertia	inersia
immediately	imediately	inference	inferance
implement	impliment	innovate	inovate
impossibly	impossiblly	insomnia	insonia
indispensable	indispensible	integrity	integrety

L

正确拼写	错误拼写	正确拼写	错误拼写
later	latter	likelihood	likelyhood
latter	later	literature	litrature

M

正确拼写	错误拼写	正确拼写	错误拼写
maintenance	maintainance	miscellaneous	misellaneous
management	managment	model	modle
miniature	miniture	monopoly	monoply

N

正确拼写	错误拼写	正确拼写	错误拼写
necessary	necesary	noticeable	noticable
necessitate	necesitate	nuisance	nusance

O

正确拼写	错误拼写	正确拼写	错误拼写
occasionally	ocasionally	opinion	opinon
occurrence	occurence	optimal	optiml
omitted	omited	original	originl

P

正确拼写	错误拼写	正确拼写	错误拼写
parallel	paralel	possess	posses
pattern	patten	preceding	preceeding
personnel	personel	privilege	privelege
phenomenon	phenomenen	professional	profesional
pivotal	pivotl	procedure	procejure
planning	planing	psychological	psycological
pneumonia	neumonia		

Q

正确拼写	错误拼写	正确拼写	错误拼写
quality	qualety	quantity	quatity
qualitative	qualitive	quantitative	quantitive

R

正确拼写	错误拼写	正确拼写	错误拼写
random	randem	recommend	recomend
really	realy	relevant	revelant
receipt	recept	relieve	releive
receive	recieve	research	reserch

S

正确拼写	错误拼写	正确拼写	错误拼写
safely	safly	sincerely	sincerly
safety	safty	substantial	substantial
scarcely	scacely	successful	succesful
separately	seperately	supersede	supercede
similar	similiar	survey	survay

T

正确拼写	错误拼写	正确拼写	错误拼写
temporal	temperal	transferred	transfered
tendency	tendancy	transient	trasient
theoretical	theoretical	twelfth	twelveth

U—Z

正确拼写	错误拼写	正确拼写	错误拼写
ultimate	ultimit	variable	varieable
useable	usable	variety	variaty
until	untill	virtually	virtully
undoutedly	undoutly	Wednesday	Wenesday
valuable	valueable	yield	yeild

4. 常见不规则变化的名词复数

analysis(单数) → analyses(复数) 分析

axis(单数) → axes(复数) 轴

bacterium(单数) → bacteria(复数) 细菌

basis(单数) → bases(复数) 基础

crisis(单数) → crises(复数) 危机

datum(单数) → data(复数) 数据

diagnosis(单数) → diagnoses(复数) 诊断

erratum(单数) → errata(复数) 错误

hypothesis(单数) → hypotheses(复数) 假说

medium(单数) → media(复数) 介质

minimum(单数) → minima(复数) 最小

parenthesis(单数) → parentheses(复数) 圆括号

phenomenon(单数) → phenomena(复数) 现象

serum(单数) → sera(复数) 血清

spectrum(单数) → spectra(复数) 光谱

stratum(单数) → strata(复数) （地）层

synthesis(单数) → syntheses(复数) 合成

thesis(单数)→ theses(复数) 毕业论文

还有一些名词有两种复数形式，如下：

appendix(单数)→appendices 或 appendixes(复数) 附录

criterion(单数)→ criteria 或 criterions(复数) 标准

formula(单数)→formulae 或 formulas(复数) 公式

focus(单数)→foci 或 focuses(复数) 焦点，焦距

radius(单数)→radii 或 radiuses(复数) 半径

terminus(单数)→ termini 或 terminuses(复数) 终点

vacuum(单数)→ vacuums 或 vacua(复数) 真空

还有几个名词单复数一样，如：

means(单数)→ means(复数) 手段

series(单数)→ series(复数) 系列

species(单数)→species(复数) 种类

5. 其他常用短语

1) 大量，许多

a considerable number of, a good many, a great deal of, a great many, a great number of, a great variety of, a large number of, a lot of, a majority of, a plenty of, a quantity of, the bulk of, the vast majority of

2) 与……对照，对比

as opposed to, as contrasted to, as compared to, by contrast, in sharp contrast to

3) 领域，范围

in the area of, in the content of, in the domain of, in the field of, in the realm of

4) 关于，就……而言

about, as far as ... be concerned, concerning, in this regard, regarding, with regard to

附录B 缩写词、数字及符号

1. 常用的缩写词

英文学术论文中会使用到许多缩写词,这些缩写词大多来自拉丁语,少部分为英语单词的缩写。表 B-1 列出常用的缩写词,可供作者在论文撰写过程中参考使用(表中未标语种的为英文单词)。

表 B-1　常用缩写词及其含义

缩写	全称	翻译
B. C.	before Christ	公元前
ca.	circa(拉丁语)	大约
cf.	confer(拉丁语)	参见
c/o	care of	由……转交
e. g.	exempli gratia(拉丁语)(= for example)	例如
et al.	et alibi	以及其他人/地方
etc.	et cetera	等等
eq.	equation	方程式
Ex.	example	例子,例如
ibid.	ibidem(拉丁语)	出处同上
id.	idem(拉丁语)	同著者
i. e.	id est(拉丁语)(= that is)	即,就是
i. c.	loco citato(拉丁语)	上述的
N. B.	nota bene(拉丁语)(= note well)	注意
ref.	reference	参考文献
via	by way of(拉丁语)	经由,经过
vice versa	拉丁语	反之亦然
viz.	videlicet(拉丁语)	即,就是说
vs.	versus(拉丁语)(= against)	……对……
v. s.	vide supra(拉丁语)	见前面所述

2. 常用符号和数字

1) 常用单位(见表 B-2)

表 B-2　常用单位

单位符号	单位名称	中文单位名称
nm	nanometer	纳米
μm	micrometer	微米
mm	millimeter	毫米
cm	centimeter	厘米
m	meter	米
mm^2	square millimeter	平方毫米
cm^2	square centimeter	平方厘米
m^2	square meter	平方米
mm^3	cubic millimeter	立方毫米
cm^3	cubic centimeter	立方厘米
m^3	cubic meter	立方米
ml	milliliter	毫升
L	liter	升
mg	milligram	毫克
g	gram	克

2）常用希腊字母

α（alpha）　　β（beta）
γ（gamma）　　δ（delta）
ε（epsilon）　　η（eta）
θ（theta）　　λ（lambda）
μ（mu）　　ν（nu）
π（pi）　　ρ（rho）
σ（sigma）　　υ（upsilon）
φ（phi）　　ψ（psi）
ω（omega）

3）幂与百分数（见表 B-3）

表 B-3　幂与百分数

数值	英语表达
67%	sixty-seven percent
10^{-8}	ten to the minus eight
10^7	ten to the seven
10^8	ten to the eighth power

4）算式中的常见符号（见表 B-4）

表 B-4　算式中的常见符号

符号	英 语 全 称	翻译
*	asterisk	星号
″	double prime	双撇
′	prime	单撇
X_m	subscript	下标
X^m	superscript	上标
≈	equivalent to	相当于
-	hyphen	连字符
∞	infinity	无限大
—	horizontal bar	水平衡杠
ln	natural logarithm	自然对数
log	common logarithm	常用对数
( )	brackets or braces	括号
[ ]	squared brackets	方括号
〈 〉	angled brackets or angled braces	角括号

5）加减乘除算式

（1）加法（addition）：加号"＋"读作 plus, add, added to, and 等；等号"＝"读作 be equal to, get, give 等，例如：

2＋5＝7　　　　　　　Two plus five equals seven.

7＋8＝15　　　　　　Seven and eight are equal to fifteen.

（2）减法（subtraction）：减号"－"读作 minus，例如：

20－6＝14　　　　　　Twenty minus six equals fourteen.

70－19＝51　　　　　Seventy minus nineteen gives fifty-one.

（3）乘法（multiplication）：乘号"×"读作 times, multiply 或 multiplied by，例如：

2.6×3＝7.8　　　　　Two point six times three equals seven point eight.

13×5＝65　　　　　　Thirteen multiplied by five is sixty-five.

（4）除法（division）：除号"÷"读作 divide, divided by，例如：

64÷4＝16　　　　　　Sixty-four divided by four equals sixteen.

9÷2＝4.5　　　　　　Divide nine by two equals four point five.

附录C 国外常见文后参考文献著录格式

简要介绍	格式示例
APA (American Psychological Association) Style 美国心理协会论文格式 该格式源于美国心理协会主办的心理学杂志，主要用于心理、教育等社会科学领域。标题的英文表述为 References	Book Author, First Initial. Middle Initial. (Year). *Book Title*. (Vols. Volume # (s)). In First Initial. Middle Initial. Editor Last Name (Ed.), Published City, Published State: Publisher. Web Document Author Last Name, First Initial. Middle Initial. (Year). In *Web Document Title*. (chap. Chapter/Section). Retrieved Month. Day, Year, from URL Address.
CMS (Chicago Manual of Style) 芝加哥手册论文格式 该格式源于芝加哥大学出版社在1906年出版的 Manual Style，现通用于编辑出版界，是美国各出版社和学术杂志对稿件要求最为常用的格式。标题的英文表述为 Bibliography	Book Author Last Name, First Name Middle Name. *Book Title*. City Published: Publisher, Year Published. Website Author Last Name, First Name Middle Name. *Site Title*. Created Day Month Year. 〈URL Address〉(Accessed Day Month Year)
CSE (Council of Science Editors) Style （美国）科学编辑理事会格式 美国科学编辑理事会前身为成立于1957年的美国生物学编辑理事会 CBE (Council of Biology Editors)，2000年 CBE 更名为 CSE。CSE Style 主要用于自然科学领域。标题的英文表述为 Cited References	Book Author Last Name, First Initial. Book Title. City Published (State Published): Publisher; Year. Total Page Numbers p. Web Document Author. Site Title [home page on the Internet]. Published City (Published State): Publisher; Year Month Day. [cited Year Month Day]. Available from: URL Address.
MLA (the Modern Language Association) Style （美国）现代语言协会论文格式 该格式是美国现代语言协会制定的书目及注释格式，多应用于语言学、文学等人文科学领域。标题的英文表述为 Works Cited	Book Author Last Name, Author First Name. <u>Book Title</u>. ed. Editor First Name Editor Last Name. City Published: Publisher, Year. Website Author Last Name, Author First Name. <u>Site Title</u>. ed. Editor First Name Last Name. Publication Day Month. Year. Accessed Day Month. Year. 〈URL Address〉.

附录D 图表的使用与语言表述

图表是学术论文的重要组成部分,是论文作者将复杂信息传递给读者最为直观、最为有效的方式。在学术论文中,常用的图表可以划分为以下九类:表格、饼形图、层面图、地图、绘图、流程与组织图、照片、折线图以及柱状图,如表 D-1 所示。

表 D-1 学术论文插图的分类、特点及其适用情况

分类及英文表述	图示	优点	适用情况
表格 (tables)	Semester / N / Mean Rank / Sum of Ranks Fall 2007 284 310.44 88164.50 Spring 2008 287 261.82 75141.50 Total 571 Spring 2008 287 247.01 70891.00 Fall 2008 159 181.07 28790.00 Total 446 Fall 2007 284 258.76 73488.00 Fall 2008 159 156.34 24858.00 Total 443	能罗列大量资料或精确数据	适用于有必要提供大量精确数据或资料,或难以表达数据的变化趋势的情况
饼形图 (pie or circle charts)	U.S. Generating Capability by Energy Source — 2003 Hydroelectric 10.5% Oil 4% Coal 33.1% Gas 22% Dual Fired 17.9% Nuclear 10.4% Other 2.1%	能清楚地显示不同项目之间量的百分比以及各项目数量与总数量之间的关系	适用于所分项目不多的场合

续表

分类及英文表述	图　示	优点	适用情况
层面图 (surface strata charts)		与多线图相似，线下面积用不同的阴影或颜色给出量的概念，当要突出量的比例或变化趋势时，层面图能更满意地表示要强调的内容	适用于平缓、有规则的变化
地图 (maps)		能直观显示地理位置和空间分布	适用于显示地理或空间的分布
绘图 (drawings and diagrams)		能有效显示设备装置的工作原理，能清楚地展示物体的内部结构	适用于表述电子线路图、机械装置图等
流程与组织图 (flow sheets and organization charts)		用符号或几何图形与连接线来表示一个过程的步骤或运行流程	适用于表述某些装置、机械部件等动态系统的工作原理、工作过程或工作状态，或用于代表一个组织内部的行政关系

续表

分类及英文表述	图 示	优点	适用情况
照片 (photographs)		能直观展示某物体的外表，具有真实性和具体性	适用于强调物体的外观而不是内部结构或剖面
折线图 (line charts)		能清楚地比较不同数据或变量在某时间段的变化	适用于展示连续性数据的变化趋势及最高点或最低点
柱状图 (bar charts)		能清楚地展示不同项目之间的关系、数量的对比，以及不同数量之间的相近或相差的关系	适用于表示不同时期的数量或大小，或同一时期内事物的大小或相对值，或整个量中各部分之间的相对大小

表 D-2　图表的语言表述

中文表达	英文表达
……到……发生急剧上升（下降）	A considerable increase/decrease occurred from … to …
……的局势到达顶（高）点，为……百分点	The situation reached a peak (a high point at) of (%)…
……的数目在……（月或年）达到顶点，为……	The figures peaked at … in … (month/year)
……年……急剧上升	(Year) witnessed/saw a sharp rise in …
……数字呈上升趋势	There is an upward trend in the number of …

续表

中 文 表 达	英 文 表 达
……(月或年)至……(月或年)……的数量基本不变	The number of … remained steady/stable from … (month/year) to … (month/year) …
……至……期间……的比率维持不变	The percentage of … stayed the same/remained stable/remained constant between … and …
……逐年减少,与此同时……逐步上升	… decreased year by year while…increased steadily
A 的比例比 B 的比例略高(低)	The percentage of A is slightly larger/smaller than that of B
A 是 B 的……倍	A is … times as much/many as B
A 与 B 有共同之处	A has something in common with B
A 与 B 的区别不大	There is not a great deal of difference between A and B
A 与 B 两者之间的关系如该表所示	The table shows the relationship between A and B
A 与 B 相似	A is similar to B
A 与 B 相同	A is the same as B
A 与 B 之间的差别在于……	The difference between A and B lies in …
A 与 B 之间有许多相似(或不同)之处	There are a lot of similarities/differences between A and B
A 增长到……	A increased to …
A 增长了……	A increased by …
X 年至 Y 年三年里……	In the 3 years spanning from X to Y …
按此趋势……	If this trend continues …
比率维持在……	The percentage remained steady at …
表 1 表明……	Table 1 shows us that …
表 1 概括了……	Table 1 summarizes …
表 1 描述了……	Table 1 represents …
表 1 清晰表明……	Table 1 shows clearly …
表 1 提示……	Table 1 suggests that …
参照该表,可以得出……	Looking at the table we can conclude that …
从……到……下降速率减慢	From … to …, the rate of decrease slowed down
从图表中,我们可以清楚地看到……	From the table/chart/diagram/figure, we can see clearly that …
从图中可以看出,……发生了巨大变化	As can be seen from the diagram, great changes have taken place in …
从这年起,……逐渐下降至……	From this year on, there was a gradual decline in the …, reaching a figure of …
该表格描述了 X 年到 Y 年间 A 与 B 的比例关系	This table shows the changing proportion of A and B from X to Y
该表格描述了在 X 年至 Y 年间……数量的变化	The table shows the changes in the number of … over the period from X to Y
该表中的数据以递减/递增呈现	The data in this table are represented in ascending/descending order
该表中第 1 列表示……	The first column of the table shows …

续表

中文表达	英文表达
该饼形图揭示了……	The pie chart depicts (that) …
该饼形图向我们揭示了如何……	The pie chart reveals how …
该数据(或数字)表明……	The data/statistics show (that) …
该图表表明……的数目增长了三倍	The graph shows a threefold increase in the number of …
该图为……	This is a graph of …
该图为我们提供了有关……的重要数据	The graph provides some important data regarding …
该图向我们展示了……	The diagram shows (that) …
该图以饼形图的形式描述了……总的趋势	The graph, presented in a pie chart, shows the general trend in …
该图中,横轴代表……,纵轴表示……	In this graph, the horizontal axis/X axis represents …, and the vertical axis/Y axis represents …
该柱状图展示了……	The bar chart illustrates that …
根据这些数字……	According to these Figures …
将表1中的数据与表2中的数据进行对比……	Comparing the data in table 1 and Table 2 …
如表1所示……	As is indicated in Table 1 …
如表格所示……	As is shown in the Table …
如图所示,两条曲线显示了……的波动情况	As can be seen from the graph, the two curves show the fluctuation of …
如图(或表)所示……	As is shown/demonstrated/exhibited in the diagram/graph/chart/Table …
如下是一个曲线图,展示了……的趋势	The following is a line chart which describes the trend of …
数据(或统计资料)表明……	The figures/statistics show (that) …
数据在……达到低点	The figures reached a low point in …
数据在……跌至谷底	The figures bottomed out in …/The figures reached the bottom in …
数字急剧上升至……	The number dramatically/sharply went up to …
图1显示……的结果为……	Figure 1 shows the result of …
在X年到Y年期间……	In the year between X and Y
在X至Y期间,……保持不变	Over the period from X to Y the …remained level
在图1中……	In Figure 1 …
该图为柱状图,描述了……	This is a bar chart showing …
该数据(或统计资料、数字)引导我们得出……结论	The data/statistics/figures lead us to the conclusion that …

附录E 学术英语写作常用词汇

A

单词	音标	词性	词义
absolute	['æbsəluːt]	adj.	完全的,十足的,绝对的,肯定的
academic	[ˌækə'demɪk]	adj.	学术的,理论的,学院的
accelerate	[ək'seləreɪt]	vt.	(使)加快,(使)增速;加速,催促;促进
		vi.	加快,加速
access	['ækses]	n.	通路,访问,入门,途径
		vt.	存取,接近
account	[ə'kaʊnt]	n.	计算,账目,说明,理由
		vi.	说明,总计有,导致
		vt.	认为
achieve	[ə'tʃiːv]	vt.	完成,达到,实现
accomplish	[ə'kʌmplɪʃ]	vt.	完成,达到,实现
accumulate	[ə'kjuːmjʊleɪt]	vt.	堆积,积累
		vi.	(数量)逐渐增加,(质量)渐渐提高
accurate	['ækjərət]	adj.	正确的,精确的
accuracy	['ækjərəsɪ]	n.	精确性,正确度
active	['æktɪv]	adj.	积极的,主动的,活跃的;现行的
activity	[æk'tɪvɪtɪ]	n.	活跃,活动性,行动,[核]放射性
actually	['æktFuəlɪ]	adv.	实际上,事实上;竟然,居然
adapt	[ə'dæpt]	vt.	使适应,改编
adaptability	[əˌdæptə'bɪlətɪ]	n.	适应性
adaptable	[ə'dæptəbl]	adj.	能适应的,可修改的
additional	[ə'dɪʃənl]	adj.	另外的,附加的,额外的
address	[ə'dres]	n.	地址;致辞,演讲;说话的技巧
		vt.	向……致辞,演说;处理;在……上写姓名地址;从事;向……提出
adequate	['ædɪkwət]	adj.	适当的,足够的
adjust	[ə'dʒʌst]	vt.	调整,调节,校准,使适合
adjustment	[ə'dʒʌstmənt]	n.	调解,调整;调节器;调解,调停;(赔偿损失的)清算
administer	[əd'mɪnɪstə(r)]	vt.	管理,治理(国家);给予;执行
		vi.	执行遗产管理人的职责,给予帮助,担当管理人
adopt	[ə'dɒpt]	vt.	采用,采纳;收养

续表

单词	音标	词性	词 义
advance	[əd'vɑːns]	n.	前进,提升,预付款
		vt.	(使)前进,将……提前,预付,提出
		vi.	(数量等)增加,向前推(至下一步),上涨
advantage	[əd'vɑːntɪdʒ]	n.	优势,有利条件,利益
advocate	['ædvəkeɪt]	n.	提倡者,鼓吹者
		vt.	提倡,鼓吹
affect	[ə'fekt]	vt.	影响,感动;感染;假装
aim	[eɪm]	n.	目标,目的
		vt. & vi.	对……瞄准,目的在于
allow	[ə'laʊ]	vt.	允许,承认
alter	['ɔːltə(r)]	vt.	改变,更改;改建(房屋);(人)变老
		vi.	改变,修改
alteration	[ˌɔːltə'reɪʃn]	n.	交替,轮流;间隔
alternative	[ɔː'tɜːnətɪv]	n.	二中择一,可供选择的办法或事
		adj.	选择性的,二中择一的
analysis	[ə'næləsɪs]	n.	分析,分解
analytical	[ˌænə'lɪtɪkl]	adj.	分析的,解析的
analyze	['ænəlaɪz]	vt.	分析,分解
apparatus	[ˌæpə'reɪtəs]	n.	器械,设备,仪器
apply	[ə'plaɪ]	vt.	申请;应用,运用
		vi.	申请,适用
applicable	[ə'plɪkəbl]	adj.	可适用的,可应用的
approach	[ə'prəʊtʃ]	n.	接近,走进;方法,步骤,途径
		vt.	接近,动手处理
		vi.	靠近
appropriate	[ə'prəʊprɪət]	adj.	适当的
approximate	[ə'prɒksɪmət]	adj.	近似的,大约的
		vt.	近似,接近,接近,约计
argue	['ɑːgjuː]	vi.	争论,辩论
		vt.	说服
artificial	[ˌɑːtɪ'fɪʃl]	adj.	人造的,不自然的,非原产地的
ascertain	[ˌæsə'teɪn]	vt.	确定,探知
aspect	['æspekt]	n.	外表,面貌;(问题等的)方面
assess	[ə'ses]	vt.	估定,评定
associate	[ə'səʊʃɪeɪt]	vt.	使发生联系,使联合
		vi.	交往,结交
		n.	合作人
attain	[ə'teɪn]	vt.	达到,获得
attempt	[ə'tempt]	n.	努力,尝试,企图
		vt.	尝试,企图
attribute	['ætrɪbjuːt]	n.	属性,品质,特征
	[ə'trɪbjuːt]	vt.	加于,归因于,归结于

续表

单词	音标	词性	词义
augment	[ɔːgˈment]	vt.	增加,增大
		n.	增加
automatic	[ˌɔːtəˈmætɪk]	n.	自动机械
		adj.	自动的,无意识的,机械的
available	[əˈveɪləbl]	adj.	可用到的,可利用的;有空的
aware	[əˈweə(r)]	adj.	知道的,明白的,意识到的
awareness	[əˈweənəs]	n.	知道,晓得

B

单词	音标	词性	词义
basic	[ˈbeɪsɪk]	adj.	基本的,主要的;碱性的
		n.	基本,要素
basically	[ˈbeɪsɪklɪ]	adv.	基本上,主要地
basis	[ˈbeɪsɪs]	n.	基础,基本,根据,主要成分(或要素),[化]基底,[医]基底、底,[经]基价
behavior	[bɪˈheɪvjə]	n.	行为,举止
beneficial	[ˌbenɪˈfɪʃl]	adj.	有益的,[经]可享利益的
benefit	[ˈbenɪfɪt]	n.	利益,[经]利益,效益,津贴
		vt.	有益于,有助于
		vi.	受益
briefly	[ˈbriːflɪ]	adv.	暂时地;简要地,简短地,简单地

C

单词	音标	词性	词义
calculate	[ˈkælkjʊleɪt]	vt.	计算;考虑,计划,打算
capable	[ˈkeɪpəbl]	adj.	有能力的,能干的;有可能的
capacity	[kəˈpæsətɪ]	n.	容量,生产量;智能,能力
case	[keɪs]	n.	病例,案例;情形;(语法)格
categorize	[ˈkætəgəraɪz]	vt.	分门别类,分类
category	[ˈkætəgərɪ]	n.	种类,[逻]范畴
cause	[kɔːz]	n.	原因,根据;目标,理想,事业
		vt.	引起,惹起,使(发生),促成
challenge	[ˈtʃælɪndʒ]	n.	挑战
		vt.	向……挑战
characteristic	[ˌkærəktəˈrɪstɪk]	adj.	特有的,表示特性的
		n.	典型的特性,特征
characterize	[ˈkærəktəraɪz]	vt.	表现……的特色;刻画,形容;定性,特性化
clarify	[ˈklærəfaɪ]	vt.	澄清,阐明
clarification	[ˌklærəfɪˈkeɪʃn]	n.	澄清,净化
classify	[ˈklæsɪfaɪ]	vt.	分类,分等
coherent	[kəʊˈhɪərənt]	adj.	粘在一起的;一致的,连贯的

续表

单词	音标	词性	词义
combine	[kəm'baɪn]	vt. & vi.	（使）联合，（使）结合
		n.	联合企业，联合收割机
compare	[kəm'peə]	vt. & vi.	比较，相比；区别；对照；比喻
comparison	[kəm'pærɪsn]	n.	比较，对照；比喻；比较关系
competence	['kɒmpɪtəns]	n.	能力
complementary	[ˌkɒmplɪ'mentri]	adj.	补充的，补足的
complex	['kɒmpleks]	adj.	复杂的，合成的，综合的
		n.	联合体
complexity	[kəm'pleksətɪ]	n.	复杂（性），复杂的事物，复杂性
complicated	['kɒmplɪkeɪtɪd]	adj.	复杂的，难解的
component	[kəm'pəʊnənt]	n.	成分
		adj.	组成的，构成的
comprise	[kəm'praɪz]	vt.	包含，由……组成
compute	[kəm'pju:t]	vt.	计算，估计，用计算机计算（或确定）
computation	[ˌkɒmpju'teɪʃn]	n.	计算，估计
conceive	[kən'si:v]	vt.	构思，以为
		vi.	怀孕；考虑，设想
concept	['kɒnsept]	n.	观念
concern	[kən'sɜ:n]	vt.	涉及，关系到
		n.	（利害）关系；关心，关注；所关心的事
conclude	[kən'klu:d]	vi.	结束，终止，决定，作出结论
		vt.	推断，断定，议定
conduct	['kɒndʌkt]	n.	行为，操行
	[kən'dʌkt]	vt.	引导，管理，行为，传导
confirm	[kən'fɜ:m]	vt.	确定，确认，批准；使巩固；使有效
consequence	['kɒnsɪkwəns]	n.	结果；推理，推论；因果关系；重要的地位
consequent	['kɒnsɪˌkwent]	adj.	作为结果的，随之发生的
consequently	['kɒnsɪkwəntli]	adv.	从而，因此
conserve	[kən'sɜ:v]	vt.	保存，保藏；保养；节约
		n.	保存，保养，保藏；防腐剂
consider	[kən'sɪdə(r)]	vt. & vi.	考虑，认为
consideration	[kənˌsɪdə'reɪʃn]	n.	体谅，考虑，需要考虑的事项
considerable	[kən'sɪdərəbl]	adj.	相当大（或多）的，相当可观的，值得考虑的
consist	[kən'sɪst]	vi.	由……组成，在于，一致
consistent	[kən'sɪstənt]	adj.	一致的，调和的；坚固的；[数、统]相容的
constant	['kɒnstənt]	n.	[数、物]常数，恒量
		adj.	不变的，持续的，坚决的
constitute	['kɒnstɪtju:t]	vt.	制定（法律），建立（政府），组成，任命
constraint	[kən'streɪnt]	n.	约束，强制，局促；限制
construct	[kən'strʌkt]	vt.	建造，构造，创立
consult	[kən'sʌlt]	vt.	商量，商议；请教；参考；考虑

续表

单词	音标	词性	词 义
contain	[kən'teɪn]	vt.	包含,容纳;容忍 自制,牵制,[数]可被……除尽
context	['kɒntekst]	n.	上下文,文章的前后关系
contrast	['kɒntrɑːst]	vt.	使与……对比,使与……对照
		vi.	和……形成对照
		n.	对比,对照,(对照中的)差异
contribute	[kən'trɪbjuːt]	vt. & vi.	捐助,捐献;贡献;投稿
control	[kən'trəʊl]	n.	控制,支配,管理;调节;抑制;控制器,调节装置
		vt.	控制,支配;管理(物价等);操纵;抑制
controversy	['kɒntrəvɜːsi]	n.	论争,辩论,论战
conventional	[kən'venʃənl]	adj.	惯例的,常规的,习俗的,传统的
converge	[kən'vɜːdʒ]	vi.	聚合,集中于一点
		vt.	会聚
convert	['kɒnvɜːt]	n.	皈依者
	[kən'vɜːt]	vt.	使转变,转换;使……改变信仰
cope	[kəʊp]	vi.	(善于)应付,(善于)处理
correlation	[ˌkɒrə'leɪʃn]	n.	相互关系,相关(性)
correspond	[ˌkɒrə'spɒnd]	vi.	符合;协调;通信;相当,相应
create	[kri'eɪt]	vt.	创造,创作;引起,造成
criterion	[kraɪ'tɪəriən]	n.	标准,准据,规范
critical	['krɪtɪkl]	adj.	评论的,鉴定的,批评的;危急的,临界,关键性的
crucial	['kruːʃl]	adj.	至关紧要的
current	['kʌrənt]	adj.	当前的,通用的,流通的,现在的,最近的
		n.	涌流,趋势,电流,水流,气流
currently	['kʌrəntli]	adv.	普遍地,通常地;现在,当前

D

单词	音标	词性	词 义
data	['deɪtə]	n.	资料,数据,材料
damage	['dæmɪdʒ]	n.	损害,赔偿金,赔偿损失,伤害
		vt.	损害
decade	['dekeɪd]	n.	十年
decay	[de'keɪ]	vi.	腐朽,腐烂;衰减,衰退
		n.	腐朽,腐烂;衰减,衰退
defect	[dɪ'fekt]	n.	缺点,缺陷
deficiency	[dɪ'fɪʃnsɪ]	n.	缺乏,不足
define	[dɪ'faɪn]	vt.	定义,规定;使明确
delay	[dɪ'leɪ]	n.	耽搁,迟滞,延时,延期,推迟
		vt.	耽搁,延迟

续表

单词	音标	词性	词 义
deliver	[dɪˈlɪvə]	vt.	递送,陈述,释放,发表,引渡,交付,交运
demand	[dɪˈmɑːnd]	n.	要求,需求,需要;销路;请求
		vt.	要求,查询
demonstrate	[ˈdemənstreɪt]	vt.	示范,证明
		vi.	示威
denote	[dɪˈnəʊt]	vt.	指示,表示
depend	[dɪˈpend]	vi.	靠,视……而定,信赖
dependent	[dɪˈpendənt]	n.	依赖他人者,[法]受扶养者,家属,依靠者
		adj.	依赖的,从属的
describe	[dɪˈskraɪb]	vt.	描述,描绘,记述;形容
design	[dɪˈzaɪn]	n.	设计,图样,方案,企图
		vt.	设计,计划
description	[dɪˈskrɪpʃən]	n.	描述,说明,[经]说明书(物品),品名种类,货物名称
derive	[dɪˈraɪv]	vt.	源自
		vi.	起源
detail	[ˈdiːteɪl]	n.	细节,详情
		vt.	详述,选派
detect	[dɪˈtekt]	vt.	发现,察觉,探测
determine	[dɪˈtɜːmɪn]	vt.	决定,决心
detrimental	[ˌdetrɪˈmentəl]	adj.	有害的
develop	[dɪˈveləp]	vt.	发展,使发达,进步,洗印,显影
		vi.	发展,生长,[医]发育;显影,显像;显层(色谱法)
development	[dɪˈveləpmənt]	n.	发展,展开,发育,开发;[医]显影,显像,显层(色谱法)
deviate	[ˈdiːvɪeɪt]	vi.	偏离,背离
device	[dɪˈvaɪs]	n.	装置,设计,设备,策略,发明物
devise	[dɪˈvaɪz]	vt.	设计,发明,图谋,遗赠给
		n.	遗赠,[法]土地遗赠,不动产遗赠
diagnosis	[ˌdaɪəgˈnəʊsɪs]	n.	诊断;调查,审察,查究;分析,判断;识别,鉴别
disadvantage	[ˌdɪsədˈvɑːntɪdʒ]	n.	缺点,不利,坏处
discipline	[ˈdɪsɪplɪn]	n.	训练,纪律;学科;[法]纪律,风纪;惩戒
		vt.	训练,惩罚
discrepancy	[dɪsˈkrepənsɪ]	n.	不符合;差异,不相符之处;矛盾;[化]不符值,偏差值
discuss	[dɪsˈkʌs]	vt.	讨论,论述,辩论
display	[dɪsˈpleɪ]	n.	显示,陈列,炫耀
		vt.	陈列,显示,表现,夸示
dissimilarity	[ˌdɪsɪmɪˈlærətɪ]	n.	不同,不一致,相异点,相异
dissolve	[dɪˈzɒlv]	vt. & vi.	溶解,液化;解散;衰减,衰退;消失;使分裂,使分解
distinct	[dɪsˈtɪŋkt]	adj.	清楚的,显著的;不同的

续表

单词	音标	词性	词 义
distribute	[dɪ'strɪbju:t]	vt.	分配,散布,分发
distribution	[ˌdɪstrə'bju:ʃən]	n.	分配;分布;分派,分发
diverge	[daɪ'vɜ:dʒ]	vi.	(道路等)分叉,(意见等)分歧,差异,脱离
diverse	[daɪ'vɜ:s]	adj.	不同的,变化多的
diversity	[daɪ'vɜ:sɪtɪ]	n.	差异,多样性
divide	[dɪ'vaɪd]	vt. & vi.	分开,分配,除,分裂
		n.	分界线,分水岭
document	['dɒkjʊmənt]	n.	文件,公文,文档,证件,证券,凭证
		vt.	证明,为……引证
domestic	[də'mestɪk]	adj.	家庭的,国内的,家用的,驯养的
dominant	['dɒmɪnənt]	adj.	占优势的,支配的,优性的,显性的
dominate	['dɒmɪneɪt]	vt.	支配,占优势
		vi.	支配,占优势
dominating	['dɒmɪneɪtɪŋ]	adj.	专横的,独裁的;主要的
drawback	['drɔ:bæk]	n.	缺点,障碍,退款,退税
dynamic	[daɪ'næmɪk]	adj.	动态的,有活力的,有力的,动力的,不断变化的
		n.	动力,动态

E

单词	音标	词性	词 义
effect	[ɪ'fekt]	n.	结果,影响,效果,效力,效应,印象,作用
		vt.	实行,引起,完成
effective	[ɪ'fektɪv]	adj.	有效的,有力的,实际的
		n.	现役兵额,实际可作战的部队,有生力量
efficiency	[ɪ'fɪʃənsɪ]	n.	效率,功效
efficient	[ɪ'fɪʃənt]	adj.	有效率的,能干的
effort	['efət]	n.	努力,成就
elaborate	[ɪ'læbərət]	adj.	精心制作的,精致的,精巧的;详细阐述的
		vt.	精心制作,详细阐述
element	['elɪmənt]	n.	元件,元素,要素,成分,单元;电池,电极,电阻丝
eliminate	[ɪ'lɪmɪneɪt]	vt.	除去,排除,剔除,消除
elucidate	[ɪ'lu:sɪdeɪt]	vt.	阐明,说明
embody	[ɪm'bɒdɪ]	vt.	具体表达,使具体化,具体表现;合并
emerge	[ɪ'mɜ:dʒ]	vi.	浮现,形成,出现,(事实)显露
emergency	[ɪ'mɜ:dʒənsɪ]	n.	紧急状况,紧急事件,紧急需要,急症,意外
emphasize	['emfəsaɪz]	vt.	强调,加强语气,着重
emphasis	['emfəsɪs]	n.	强调,重点
empirical	[em'pɪrɪkəl]	adj.	经验的;实验的;完全根据经验的,经验主义的
employ	[ɪm'plɔɪ]	n.	雇用
		vt.	雇用,使用,使从事于,采用
enable	[ɪ'neɪbl]	vt.	使能够,给予能力,赋予权力,使……运作,激活
enhance	[ɪn'hɑ:ns]	vt.	提高,加强,增加

续表

单词	音标	词性	词义
enormous	[ɪˈnɔːməs]	adj.	巨大的,庞大的
ensure	[ɪnˈʃʊə]	vt.	确定,保证,担保,保护
entirely	[ɪnˈtaɪəlɪ]	adv.	完全,全然,一概
environment	[ɪnˈvaɪrənmənt]	n.	环境,外界,围绕
equip	[ɪˈkwɪp]	vt.	装备,配备,设备,装置
equipment	[ɪˈkwɪpmənt]	n.	装备,设备;才能,装置,器材
error	[ˈerə]	n.	错误,过失,误差
essential	[ɪˈsenʃəl]	n.	要素,要点;本质
		adj.	必要的,重要的,本质的;[医]必需的;自发的;特发的
establish	[ɪˈstæblɪʃ]	vt.	建立,确立;制定,设立;安置,使定居
		vi.	(植物等)移植生长
estimate	[ˈestɪmeɪt]	n.	估计,判断
		vt. & vi.	估计,评价,判断,预估
estimation	[ˌestɪˈmeɪʃən]	n.	估计,预算,评价,判断
evaluate	[ɪˈvæljʊeɪt]	vt.	评价,估计,求……的值
evaluation	[ɪˌvæljʊˈeɪʃən]	n.	评估,评价,估价,求值;鉴定
eventually	[ɪˈventʃʊəlɪ]	adv.	最后,终于
evidence	[ˈevɪdəns]	n.	根据,证据,迹象,凭证
evident	[ˈevɪdənt]	adj.	显然的,明显的
examine	[ɪgˈzæmɪn]	vt.	调查,考试;检验,检查,审查,验证
exceed	[ɪkˈsiːd]	vt.	超过,超越,胜过
exception	[ɪkˈsepʃən]	n.	例外,除外;异议,异常
exclude	[ɪksˈkluːd]	vt.	除外;排除,排斥
exhaustive	[ɪgˈzɔːstɪv]	adj.	消耗的,枯竭的;彻底的,详尽的
exhibit	[ɪgˈzɪbɪt]	n.	展览,展品;证物
		vt.	展现,陈列,展览,展示;显示
experience	[ɪkˈspɪərɪəns]	n.	经历,经验,阅历
		vt.	经历,经验,体验
experiment	[ɪkˈsperɪmənt]	n.	实验,试验;实验仪器
		vi.	实验,尝试
experimental	[ɪkˌsperɪˈmentəl]	adj.	实验的,根据实验的
expense	[ɪkˈspens]	n.	费用,开支;代价,损失
explain	[ɪkˈspleɪn]	vt.	解释,说明
exploit	[ˈeksplɔɪt]	n.	功绩,勋绩
		vt.	开发,利用,开拓,开采;剥削
explore	[ɪkˈsplɔː]	vt. & vi.	探险,探测,探究;勘探研究
extend	[ɪkˈstend]	vt. & vi.	扩充,延伸,伸展,扩大,蔓延(指病变)
extensive	[ɪkˈstensɪv]	adj.	广的,广泛的,多方面的;广大的,扩大的
extensively	[ɪkˈstensɪvlɪ]	adv.	广泛地;广阔地,大面积地
external	[ɪkˈstɜːnl]	n.	外部,外面
		adj.	外部的,客观的,表面的,外面的,外界的

F

单词	音标	词性	词 义
facilitate	[fə'sɪlɪteɪt]	vt.	使容易,促进,帮助,使便利,推进
factor	['fæktə]	n.	因素,因数,系数;代理人;要素
feasible	['fi:zəbl]	adj.	可行的,切实可行的
feature	['fi:tʃə]	n.	面孔的一部分(如眼、口等),容貌;特征,特色;特写
		vt.	是……的特色,特写,放映
		vi.	起重要作用
feedback	['fi:dbæk]	n.	反馈,反应,回复;反作用;反馈效应
financial	[faɪ'nænʃl]	adj.	财政的,金融的
flexible	['fleksəbl]	adj.	灵活的,柔顺的;易曲的;能变形的;可通融的
flexibility	[fleksɪ'bɪlɪtɪ]	n.	弹性;适应性;灵活性;柔韧性,柔曲性
focus	['fəʊkəs]	n.	焦点,焦距,疫源地
		vi.	聚焦,注视
		vt.	使聚焦,调焦,集中
form	[fɔ:m]	n.	形状,形体;类型;方式;表格;形式
		vt.	形成,排列,(使)组成
format	['fɔ:mæt]	n.	开本,版式,形式,格式
		vt.	格式化
former	['fɔ:mə]	adj.	从前的,前者的
		n.	起形成作用的人(或物),模型,样板,成形器
formula	['fɔ:mjʊlə]	n.	客套语,公式,准则,处方
formulate	['fɔ:mjʊleɪt]	vt.	用公式表示;明确地叙述,阐明;制订
framework	['freɪmwɜ:k]	n.	结构,骨架;参照标准,准则;观点;构架组织
frequency	['fri:kwənsɪ]	n.	频率,频数
frequently	['fri:kwəntlɪ]	adv.	频繁,经常地
fulfill	[fʊl'fɪl]	vt.	履行,实现,完成(计划等);遵守
function	['fʌŋkʃən]	n.	官能,职务,功能;函数
		vi.	活动,运行,行使职责
fundamental	[fʌndə'mentəl]	n.	基本原理;原则
		adj.	基本的,重要的,必要的,根本的

G

单词	音标	词性	词 义
gain	[geɪn]	n.	增益,获得,利润,收获,增加
		vt.	得到,增进,赚到
		vi.	获利,增加,上涨,上扬
gap	[gæp]	n.	缝隙,缺口,裂口,隔阂,差距,间断,间距,空隙
generate	['dʒenəreɪt]	vt.	产生,发生,创造,生成
genuine	['dʒenjʊɪn]	adj.	真实的,真正的,诚恳的
global	['gləʊbl]	adj.	球形的;全球的,全世界的;综合的;完全的,全局的,全面的;总括的;普遍的

续表

单词	音标	词性	词义
goal	[gəʊl]	n.	目标,终点,得分,球门
		vi.	攻门,得分
govern	['gʌvən]	vt. & vi.	统治,支配,管理
guarantee	[ˌgærən'tiː]	n.	担保,抵押品;保证书
		vt.	保证,担保

H

单词	音标	词性	词义
handle	[hændl]	n.	柄,把手;把柄;柄状物,手感
		vt.	运用,买卖,处理,操作
hardware	['hɑːdweə]	n.	五金器具,(电脑的)硬件,(电子仪器的)部件
highlight	['haɪlaɪt]	n.	加亮区,精彩场面
		vt.	加亮,使显著;以强光照射;突出,[经]重点新闻
hypothesis	[haɪ'pɒθəsɪs]	n.	假设,假说

I

单词	音标	词性	词义
identical	[aɪ'dentɪkəl]	adj.	同一的;恒等的;同等的,完全相同的
identify	[aɪ'dentɪfaɪ]	vt.	识别,认为……等同于,确定,使参与
		vi.	一致,认同
illustrate	['ɪləstreɪt]	vt.	举例说明,作图解,阐明
impact	['ɪmpækt]	n.	冲击,冲突;影响;效果
		vt.	挤入,撞击,压紧,对……发生影响
implement	['ɪmplɪmənt]	n.	工具,器具;手段
		vt.	实现;使生效;执行,贯彻,履行,施行
imply	[ɪm'plaɪ]	vt.	暗示,意味,隐含
important	[ɪm'pɔːtənt]	adj.	重要的,有地位的,大量的,显要的
improve	[ɪm'pruːv]	vt.	改良,提高……的价值,改善,利用
		vi.	变得更好,增加
include	[ɪn'kluːd]	vt.	包括,把……算入,包含
incorporate	[ɪn'kɔːpəreɪt]	adj.	合并的,组成公司的,一体化的
		vt.	吸收,合并,混合,使组成公司
		vi.	合并,混合;组成公司
indicate	['ɪndɪkeɪt]	vt.	显示,象征,指示,指出
indispensable	[ˌɪndɪs'pensəbl]	n.	不可缺少之物
		adj.	不可缺少的,责无旁贷的,绝对必要的
individual	[ˌɪndɪ'vɪdʒʊəl]	n.	人,个人,个体
		adj.	个别的,个人的,独特的,独立的
inevitably	[ɪn'evɪtəblɪ]	adv.	不可避免地
infer	[ɪn'fɜː(r)]	vt.	推论出,推断,作推论
inference	['ɪnfərəns]	n.	推论,推理,推断

续表

单词	音标	词性	词 义
influence	[ˈɪnfluəns]	n.	影响力;权力,势力
		vt.	影响,改变
information	[ˌɪnfəˈmeɪʃən]	n.	消息;知识;通知;情报,资料,信息
inhibit	[ɪnˈhɪbɪt]	vt.	抑制,限制;约束;禁止,阻止
initial	[ɪˈnɪʃl]	adj.	最初的,初始的;词首的
		n.	词首大写字母
innovate	[ˈɪnəveɪt]	vi.	改革,创新
insight	[ˈɪnsaɪt]	n.	洞悉,洞察力;自知力;见识
inspect	[ɪnˈspekt]	vt.	检查,检阅,检验
inspection	[ɪnˈspekʃən]	n.	检验,检查;视察,监督,审查;望诊
integrate	[ˈɪntɪgreɪt]	vt. & vi.	综合;使完整,使成整体
		adj.	完整的,完全的
intend	[ɪnˈtend]	vt.	计划,打算,想要;意指
intensive	[ɪnˈtensɪv]	adj.	加强的,内涵的,集中的
		n.	加强器
interaction	[ˌɪntərˈækʃən]	n.	交互作用,交感,相互作用
internal	[ɪnˈtɜːnəl]	adj.	内在的,国内的,内部的
interpret	[ɪnˈtɜːprɪt]	vt.	解释,翻译,理解
introduce	[ˌɪntrəˈdjuːs]	vt.	介绍,引入,采用,输入
invest	[ɪnˈvest]	vt.	投资,授予
investigate	[ɪnˈvestɪgeɪt]	v.	调查,审查
investigation	[ɪnˌvestɪˈgeɪʃən]	n.	调查,审查,调查研究
involve	[ɪnˈvɒlv]	vt.	包括,使陷于,潜心于,包围,牵涉,包含
issue	[ˈɪʃuː]	n.	发行,问题,后果,流出,出口,争端
		vi.	发行,流出,造成……结果
		vt.	使流出,放出,发行,发布,发给

K

单词	音标	词性	词 义
key	[kiː]	n.	钥匙;键,关键,线索,秘诀;解答,答案;基调
		vt.	调音,锁上,提供线索
		vi.	使用钥匙
		adj.	关键的,主要的

L

单词	音标	词性	词 义
latter	[ˈlætə]	adj.	后者的,较后的;近来的
launch	[lɔːntʃ]	vt. & vi.	使下水;发射;发动,起飞,开始
		n.	下水,汽艇,发射
likelihood	[ˈlaɪklɪhud]	n.	可能,可能性
likely	[ˈlaɪklɪ]	adj.	有可能的,可靠的,合适的,前途有望的
		adv.	或许;大概;很可能

续表

单词	音标	词性	词义
limit	[ˈlɪmɪt]	n.	界限,边界;限度;极限;限制
		vt.	限制,限定,界限,限价
literature	[ˈlɪtərətʃə]	n.	文献,文学,文艺,著作
local	[ˈləukəl]	adj.	地方性的;当地的,本地的;局部的;乡土的
		n.	当地居民,本地新闻,局部,当地交货,当场交货价
logic	[ˈlɒdʒɪk]	n.	逻辑,逻辑学,推理的方法,推理,逻辑性

M

单词	音标	词性	词义
maintain	[meɪnˈteɪn]	vt.	维持;维修;保持;坚持;供养;主张
maintenance	[ˈmeɪntənəns]	n.	维护,保持,维修;生活费用;坚持;保养(费),维护(费)
major	[ˈmeɪdʒə]	adj.	主要的;较多的,大部分的;成年的
		vi.	主修
		n.	主修课,成年人,陆军少校
majority	[məˈdʒɒrɪti]	n.	多数,大半,大多数
manage	[ˈmænɪdʒ]	vi.	处理
		vt.	管理,控制,维持;达成;经营;运用
management	[ˈmænɪdʒmənt]	n.	经营;支配,管理;管理处,董事会
manipulate	[məˈnɪpjuleɪt]	vt.	操纵,利用,操作;巧妙地处理;假造
maximize	[ˈmæksɪmaɪz]	vt.	取最大值,使增加(或扩大)到最大限度,最大化
maximum	[ˈmæksɪməm]	n.	极点,最大量,最大值,极大
		adj.	最高的,最大的,最大极限的
measure	[ˈmeʒə]	n.	尺寸,量度标准;测量;程度,范围,限度,分寸;措施,方法;量度器,量具
		vt.	测量,测度,估量,权衡,调节
		vi.	度量
method	[ˈmeθəd]	n.	方法,办法;条理,秩序
methodology	[ˌmeθəˈdɒlədʒɪ]	n.	方法学,方法论;操作法,工艺
minimize	[ˈmɪnɪmaɪz]	vt.	将……减到最少,最小化
minimum	[ˈmɪnɪməm]	adj.	最小的,最低的
		n.	最小值,最小,最低,最低点,最小量,最低量,最低数
minor	[ˈmaɪnə]	adj.	较小的,二流的,未成年的,次要的
		vi.	副修,选修
		n.	未成年人;副修科目
minority	[maɪˈnɒrɪtɪ]	n.	少数,未成年,少数民族
		adj.	少数的,少数派的
model	[ˈmɒdl]	n.	模型,模范;模特儿;典型,样品
		vi.	做模型,做模特儿
		vt.	使模仿,塑造

续表

单词	音标	词性	词 义
moderate	[ˈmɒdərət]	adj.	有节制的；稳健的,温和的；适度的,中等的
		vt.	节制,减轻,使缓和
		vi.	变缓和,主持会议
modify	[ˈmɒdɪfaɪ]	vt.	修改,修饰；更改,变更；缓和,减轻
modification	[ˌmɒdɪfɪˈkeɪʃən]	n.	更改；修改,修正；调整
monitor	[ˈmɒnɪtə]	n.	监督器,级长,监视员,班长,监视器,告诫物,监测器,监控器,监护员
		vt.	监视,监听；监督
motivation	[ˌməʊtɪˈveɪʃən]	n.	动机,刺激,推动,促动,诱导

N

单词	音标	词性	词 义
necessary	[ˈnesəsərɪ]	adj.	必需的,需要的；必然的,不可缺少的
		n.	（通常用复数）（生活）必需品
necessitate	[nɪˈsesɪteɪt]	vt.	迫使,使成为必需,需要
neglect	[nɪˈglekt]	n.	疏忽,忽略,漏做
		vt.	疏忽,忽视,忽略
network	[ˈnetwɜːk]	n.	网络,网状物,广播网
novel	[ˈnɒvl]	n.	小说,长篇故事
		adj.	新奇的,异常的

O

单词	音标	词性	词 义
objective	[əbˈdʒektɪv]	n.	目的,目标,宗旨；宾格；实物
		adj.	客观的,如实的,无偏见的；宾格的
observation	[ˌɒbzɜːˈveɪʃən]	n.	观察,注意,观测,观察力
observe	[əbˈzɜːv]	vt.	遵守,观察,庆祝
		vi.	注意,评论,观察
obtain	[əbˈteɪn]	vt.	获得
		vi.	流行,得到公认
occur	[əˈkɜː]	vi.	发生,出现,存在
offer	[ˈɒfə]	n.	给予（物）,出价,提议,意图
		vt.	提供,出价,奉献,试图
		vi.	出现,献祭,提议,求婚
operate	[ˈɒpəreɪt]	vi.	操作,工作；运转；起作用
		vt.	（药物等）奏效；施手术；[军]作战；操纵市场
operation	[ˌɒpəˈreɪʃn]	n.	运转,操作,实施,作用,工作；手术；军事行动
optimal	[ˈɒptɪməl]	adj.	最佳的,最理想的,最优的,最适的,最适当的
optimize	[ˈɒptɪmaɪz]	vt.	使完美,使完善；充分利用；乐观地对待；优化
		vi.	持乐观态度
optimization	[ˌɒptɪmaɪˈzeɪʃən]	n.	最佳化,最优化

续表

单词	音标	词性	词 义
organize	[ˈɔːɡənaɪz]	vt.	组织,有机化,给予生机
		vi.	组织起来
original	[əˈrɪdʒnəl]	adj.	最初的,原始的;有创意的
		n.	原物,原作,正本
outcome	[ˈaʊtkʌm]	n.	结果,成果,结局;出路

P

单词	音标	词性	词 义
paper	[ˈpeɪpə]	n.	纸;文件,文章,报纸;证券,证件
		vt.	用纸糊,贴壁纸于,用纸包装
		adj.	纸做的,纸上的;有名无实的
parameter	[pəˈræmɪtə]	n.	参变数,参变量,参数,参量
paramount	[ˈpærəmaʊnt]	n.	首长,最高当局
		adj.	最重要的,最高的,至上的;首要的
participate	[pɑːˈtɪsɪpeɪt]	vt. & vi.	参加,参与;分享,分担
passive	[ˈpæsɪv]	adj.	消极的,被动的,冷漠的;顺从的;无利息的
pattern	[ˈpætən]	n.	模范,典型,式样,样品,图案,格调,模式
		vt.	模仿,仿造;以图案装饰
		vi.	形成图案
perform	[pəˈfɔːm]	vt.	进行,履行,完成,执行;表演
		vi.	行动,演出
performance	[pəˈfɔːməns]	n.	履行,执行;成绩;性能;表演,演奏
phenomenon	[fɪˈnɒmɪnən]	n.	现象,迹象,表现;奇迹,奇才;征兆
pilot	[ˈpaɪlət]	n.	飞行员,领航员,航船者;导向器,驾驶仪;向导;领导人
		vt.	领航,驾驶,引导;试用
		adj.	引导的,控制的,试点的
pivotal	[ˈpɪvətl]	adj.	关键的,中枢的,枢轴的
plan	[plæn]	n.	计划,方案,规划,策略,方法;进度表,程序表,平面图,设计图,轮廓,示意图
		vt.	计划,设计,意欲
potential	[pəˈtenʃəl]	n.	潜在性,可能性;潜力,潜能
		adj.	有潜力的,可能的,潜在的
practical	[ˈpræktɪkl]	adj.	实际的,现实的,实用性的,事实上的,实际上的
practice	[ˈpræktɪs]	n.	实践,练习;惯例,习惯;开业
		vt.	实践,实行,练习,实习
precise	[prɪˈsaɪs]	adj.	精确的,严谨的,明确的,精密的,正确的
precision	[prɪˈsɪʒən]	n.	精密,精确,精确度,精度
predict	[prɪˈdɪkt]	vt.	预知,预言,预报
prediction	[prɪˈdɪkʃən]	n.	预言,预报,预测
predictable	[prɪˈdɪktəbl]	adj.	可预言的

续表

单词	音标	词性	词义
preference	['prefrəns]	n.	偏爱,优先选择
present	['preznt]	n.	现在,礼品
		adj.	现在的,出席的,目前的
		vt.	介绍,引见;赠送;提出;呈现;上演
previous	['pri:vɪəs]	adj.	早先的,前面的,过早的,以前的,先前的,前述的
preliminary	[prɪ'lɪmɪnərɪ]	n.	初步做法,初步措施;预试,预选赛
		adj.	初步的,开始的,预备的,前驱的,开端的
primary	['praɪmərɪ]	n.	最主要者,原色
		adj.	主要的;初级的,根本的,原始的;首要的,基本的
primarily	['praɪmərɪlɪ]	adv.	主要地,首先地
principal	['prɪnsɪpəl]	n.	校长,首长,本金,主犯,资本,委托人
		adj.	主要的,最重要的,首要的
principle	['prɪnsɪpl]	n.	原则,原理;主义;成分,要素
pior	['praɪə]	adj.	更重要的;较早的,在先的,在……之前
probe	[prəub]	n.	探索,调查;探针,探测器
		vt.	用探针探测,调查,探索
procedure	[prə'si:dʒə]	n.	程序,手续,方法,步骤,措施;行动,处置
process	['prəuses]	n.	程序,进行,处理,过程
		vt. & vi.	加工,使……接受处理,对……处置,列队行进
		adj.	经过特殊加工的
productivity	[ˌprɒdʌk'tɪvətɪ]	n.	生产力
profit	['prɒfɪt]	n.	利润,赢利,利益
		vi.	有益;获利,赚钱
		vt.	有益于
prominent	['prɒmɪnənt]	adj.	卓越的,突出的;显著的;凸出的
profound	[prə'faund]	adj.	极深的,深厚的;深刻的,渊博的
programme	['prəugræm]	n.	节目,节目单;程序;纲要,大纲;计划
		vt.	规划,拟……计划
		vi.	安排节目,编程序
project	['prɒdʒekt]	n.	计划,设计,事业,项目,方案
		vt.	计划,设计;投掷,发射;使凸出;放映
		vi.	凸出
promote	[prə'məut]	vt.	促进,晋升,推销,推广
property	['prɒpətɪ]	n.	财产;所有权;性质,性能,属性
proposal	[prə'pəuzl]	n.	提案,提议,计划;求婚;申请;投标
propose	[prə'pəuz]	vt.	计划,打算;建议,提议;求(婚)
		vi.	打算,求婚
prove	[pru:v]	vt.	证明,查验,检验,勘探,显示
		vi.	证明是,显示出
provide	[prə'vaɪd]	vt.	提供,供应,规定;预备
		vi.	做准备,抚养,规定

续表

单词	音标	词性	词义
purchase	[ˈpɜːtʃəs]	vt.	买,购买,购置;赢得
		n.	买,购买
purpose	[ˈpɜːpəs]	n.	目的,意向,用途
		vt.	意欲,企图

Q

单词	音标	词性	词义
quality	[ˈkwɒləti]	n.	品质,性质,特性;才能;质量
		adj.	优质的,高质量的
qualify	[ˈkwɒlɪfaɪ]	vt.	(使)具有资格,证明合格;限制修饰,限制,限定
quantify	[ˈkwɒntɪfaɪ]	vt.	定量,用数量表示
qualitative	[ˈkwɒlɪtətɪv]	adj.	性质的,质的,定性的
quantitative	[ˈkwɒntɪtətɪv]	adj.	数量的,定量的

R

单词	音标	词性	词义
random	[ˈrændəm]	n.	随意,随机
		adj.	任意的,随便的,胡乱的,随机的,无原则的,随意选择的
range	[reɪndʒ]	vt.	排列,归类于,使并列;放牧
		vi.	平行,延伸,漫游
		n.	量程,范围,域,幅度
react	[rɪˈækt]	vi.	起反应,起作用;反攻
reaction	[rɪˈækʃən]	n.	反应,反作用,反动
recent	[ˈriːsnt]	adj.	最近的,近代的,最新的,新进的
recommend	[ˌrekəˈmend]	vt.	推荐;介绍;劝告;使受欢迎;托付
reflect	[rɪˈflekt]	vt.	反射,反映,深思
		vi.	反射,映出;深思,考虑
regional	[ˈriːdʒənl]	adj.	地区性的,地域性的
regular	[ˈregjʊlə]	adj.	规则的,常例的,有秩序的,整齐的;等边的;定期的,经常的;合格的;正式的;固定的
		n.	正规军,正式队员
relationship	[rɪˈleɪʃənʃɪp]	n.	关系,关联
relative	[ˈrelətɪv]	n.	亲戚,关系词
		adj.	有关系的,相对的,比较的
relatively	[ˈrelətɪvli]	adv.	相对地,比较地,相当地,相关地
relevant	[ˈrelɪvənt]	adj.	有关联的,有关系的;适当的,相应的,相关的
reliability	[rɪˌlaɪəˈbɪlɪti]	n.	信度,可靠性
reliable	[rɪˈlaɪəbl]	adj.	可靠的,可信赖的,确实的
rely	[rɪˈlaɪ]	vi.	信赖,依赖,信任
remarkable	[rɪˈmɑːkəbl]	adj.	不平常的,值得注意的,显著的

续表

单词	音标	词性	词义
remedy	['remɪdɪ]	n.	治疗法,治疗;补救,赔偿
		vt.	治疗;补救;矫正,改善;修补,修缮;补偿,赔偿
report	[rɪ'pɔːt]	n.	报告,报道,传说,案情报告,爆炸声,成绩单
		vt.	报告,汇报,转述,报道;揭发;使报到
		vi.	报告,写报道,报到
represent	[ˌreprɪ'zent]	vt.	表现,表示,描绘,代表,象征;再赠送,再上演
		vi.	提出异议
require	[rɪ'kwaɪə]	vt.	需要,命令,要求
requirement	[rɪ'kwaɪəmənt]	n.	需求,必要条件,要求
research	[rɪ'sɜːtʃ]	n.	研究,调查,考察
		vi.	研究,调查
resolve	[rɪ'zɒlv]	vi.	解决,分解,决心
		vt.	使分解,解析;解决,消除;决心
		n.	决定之事,决心,坚决
resource	[rɪ'sɔːs]	n.	资源;财力;办法,策略,机智
response	[rɪ'spɒns]	n.	反应,回答,响应
responsible	[rɪ'spɒnsəbl]	adj.	有责任的,负责的,责任重大的,应负责任的,能履行责任的
responsibility	[rɪˌspɒnsə'bɪlɪtɪ]	n.	责任,职责,负担
result	[rɪ'zʌlt]	n.	结果,成绩,效果
		vi.	产生,结果,致使
reveal	[rɪ'viːl]	vt.	露出,显示,透露,揭露,泄露,(神)启示
role	[rəʊl]	n.	角色,职责,任务,作用,功用

S

单词	音标	词性	词义
salient	['seɪlɪənt]	adj.	显著的,突出的;跳跃的
		n.	凸角,突出部分
safety	['seɪftɪ]	n.	安全,保险;安全设备,保险装置
scale	[skeɪl]	n.	刻度,衡量,比例,比例尺;数值范围,等级,规模;天平
		vt.	依比例决定;攀登;测量,绘制;过秤
		vi.	剥落,生水垢,重量为,攀登,衡量
schedule	['ʃedjuːl]	vt.	预定,编制目录,制……表,安排
		n.	时间表,一览表,计划表,议事日程
scheme	[skiːm]	n.	安排,配置,计划,阴谋;方案
		vt. & vi.	计划,设计;图谋,策划
secondary	['sekəndərɪ]	adj.	中级的,中等的,次要的,第二的,从属的,辅助的
seek	[siːk]	vt.	寻求,寻找,探索,追求;搜索
		vi.	寻找,搜索

续表

单词	音标	词性	词　　义
select	[sɪˈlekt]	adj.	挑选出来的，极好的
		vt.	选择，挑选
sequence	[ˈsiːkwəns]	n.	序列，顺序；续发事件，连续，接续
		vt.	按顺序排好
shift	[ʃɪft]	n.	变化，移动，轮班，移位
		vt.	替换，转移，改变，推卸，变速
show	[ʃəʊ]	n.	出示，表现；展览；卖弄，炫耀；外观
		vt.	表示，显示，展现；陈列；演出；表明，指出
		vi.	露面，显现；演出
significant	[sɪgˈnɪfɪkənt]	adj.	重要的，有效的，有含义的，值得注意的
similar	[ˈsɪmɪlə]	adj.	相似的，类似的
simulate	[ˈsɪmjʊleɪt]	vt.	模拟，模仿；假装，冒充
simulation	[ˌsɪmjʊˈleɪʃn]	n.	仿真，假装，模拟
situation	[ˌsɪtjʊˈeɪʃən]	n.	情形，境遇；位置；情境，处境
software	[ˈsɒftweə(r)]	n.	软件
solution	[səˈluːʃn]	n.	解决，解答；溶液
source	[sɔːs]	n.	来源，水源，根源，原始资料
solve	[sɒlv]	vt.	解决，解答，解释
spatial	[ˈspeɪʃəl]	adj.	空间的，受空间条件限制的，占地位的
specialize	[ˈspeʃəlaɪz]	vt. & vi.	专攻，专门研究；使适应特殊目的，使专用于
specify	[ˈspesɪfaɪ]	vt.	详列；指定；说明，详细说明
specific	[spɪˈsɪfɪk]	n.	特效药，特性
		adj.	特殊的，明确的，特有的，特定的，具有特效的
stability	[stəˈbɪlɪtɪ]	n.	安定，稳定性，坚实，巩固
stage	[steɪdʒ]	n.	阶段，舞台，场所，戏剧，驿站，级，脚手架
		vt.	上演，表演；筹划
		vi.	上演，乘驿车旅行
standard	[ˈstændəd]	n.	标准，规格；军旗；本位
		adj.	标准的，合规格的
statistics	[stəˈtɪstɪks]	n.	统计学；统计资料，统计信息
statistical	[stəˈtɪstɪkl]	adj.	统计的，统计上的，统计学的
status	[ˈsteɪtəs]	n.	状态，情形；地位；身份
stem	[stem]	n.	茎，干，柄；船首；血统；堵塞物
		vt.	摘掉茎，装柄于，阻止
		vi.	源自，起源于；堵住；逆行
strategy	[ˈstrætɪdʒɪ]	n.	战略，策略
structure	[ˈstrʌktʃə]	n.	结构，构造；建筑物
		vt.	构成，组织

续表

单词	音标	词性	词 义
study	['stʌdɪ]	n.	学习,研究,求学,书房,试作
		vt.	学习,读书,研究,考虑,计划
		vi.	学习,思索
subject	['sʌbdʒekt]	n.	科目,主题,臣民,主语,题目,(事物的)经受者,受治疗者,受试者,受验者
		adj.	服从的,易患……的,隶属的,受支配的
		vt.	使隶属,使受到
subsequent	['sʌbsɪkwənt]	adj.	后来的,接下去的
substantial	[səb'stænʃəl]	n.	重要材料(或事物),有实际价值的东西
		adj.	实质上的,物质的,有内容的;结实的;巨大的
suggest	[sə'dʒest]	vt.	提议,建议,促成;暗示,启发,使人想起
suitable	['sjuːtəbl]	adj.	适当的,相配的,合适的,适宜的
summarize	['sʌməraɪz]	vt.	概述,总结
supply	[sə'plaɪ]	n.	补给,供给,供应品
		vt.	补给,供给,提供,补充
		vi.	替代
support	[sə'pɔːt]	n.	支持,支撑,援助,供养,支撑物
		vt.	支援,支撑,帮助,支持;供养;证实
survey	[sə'veɪ]	n.	纵览,视察,测量,观测,俯瞰,检查,调查
		vt.	审视,视察,俯瞰,通盘考虑
		vi.	测量土地
survive	[sə'vaɪv]	vt.	幸免于,幸存,生还
sustainable	[sə'steɪnəbl]	adj.	足可支撑的,养得起的,可以忍受的,可持续的
synthesis	['sɪnθəsɪs]	n.	综合,合成,综合物
system	['sɪstəm]	n.	系统,体系,制度;方式,秩序;学派

T

单词	音标	词性	词 义
target	['tɑːgɪt]	n.	目标,靶子
		vt.	对准,定指标
task	[tɑːsk]	n.	工作,任务,作业;苦差事
		vt.	派给……工作,使辛劳
technical	['teknɪkl]	adj.	技术上的,工艺的,专门性的
technique	[tek'niːk]	n.	技巧,技术,方法,工艺方法,方法技能
technology	[tek'nɒlədʒɪ]	n.	技术,工艺,工业技术;技术学,工艺学
temporal	['tempərəl]	adj.	时间的,暂时的,现世的,世俗的
		n.	世间万物,暂存的事物
tendency	['tendənsɪ]	n.	趋向,倾向,趋势
tentative	['tentətɪv]	n.	试验;假设
		adj.	试验性的;暂时的,暂定的;假定的,尝试的

续表

单词	音标	词性	词 义
test	[test]	n.	测试,试验,化验,检验,考验
		vt.	测试,试验,化验
		vi.	接受测验,进行测试
theoretical	[ˌθɪəˈretɪkl]	adj.	理论的,理论上的;假设的,推理的
theory	[ˈθɪəri]	n.	理论,学说;原理;推测
thorough	[ˈθʌrə]	adj.	十分的,彻底的
traditional	[trəˈdɪʃnl]	adj.	传统的,惯例的
trait	[treɪt]	n.	特征,特性;少许
transaction	[trænˈsækʃən]	n.	交易,办理;学报;和解协议;事务处理,交易事项
transient	[ˈtrænziənt]	n.	短期居留者,过境鸟,瞬变现象,过渡过程
		adj.	短暂的,易变的,瞬变的;路过的
transparency	[trænsˈpærənsi]	n.	透明,透明度,幻灯片
trend	[trend]	n.	趋势,倾向,走向
		vt. & vi.	倾向,转向
typical	[ˈtɪpɪkl]	adj.	典型的,象征性的

U

单词	音标	词性	词 义
ultimate	[ˈʌltɪmət]	n.	终极,根本,顶点,基本原则
		adj.	终极的,根本的,极限的,最远的,最后的,最大的
undertake	[ˌʌndəˈteɪk]	vt.	承担,担任,从事,着手,进行;许诺,保证
uniform	[ˈjuːnɪfɔːm]	adj.	统一的,相同的,一致的,均衡的
		n.	制服
		vt.	使成一样,使穿制服
use	[juːz]	n.	使用,使用价值,用法,使用权
		vt	使用,利用,运用;耗费
utilize	[ˈjuːtɪlaɪz]	vt.	利用,采用,应用

V

单词	音标	词性	词 义
valid	[ˈvælɪd]	adj.	有效的,有根据的;正当的,正确的
validate	[ˈvælɪdeɪt]	vt.	使有效,使生效;确认,证实,验证
value	[ˈvæljuː]	n.	价值,价格,购买力;重要性
		vt.	评价,估价,重视
variable	[ˈveəriəbl]	n.	易变的事物,变数,可变物,可变参数,变量
		adj.	可变的,不定的,易变的,变量的
variety	[vəˈraɪəti]	n.	变化,品种,多样,种类,变种
various	[ˈveəriəs]	adj.	不同的,多方面的,许多的,杂色的,各式各样的
vary	[ˈveəri]	vt.	改变,使多样化
		vi.	变化;有不同;违反;变换,交替

续表

单词	音标	词性	词 义
verify	['verɪfaɪ]	vt.	证明,查证,证实;检验,校验,核对
virtually	['vɜːtʃʊəlɪ]	adv.	事实上
vital	['vaɪtl]	adj.	生命的,重要的;充满活力的;生死攸关的,紧要的

Y

单词	音标	词性	词 义
yield	[jiːld]	n.	生产量,收益
		vt.	出产;给予,让出;放弃,使屈服
		vi.	屈服,投降,倒塌;产生,结果实

参考文献

Allison D. 1999. Key concepts in ELT[J]. ELT Journal, 53 (2): 144.

Allison D. 2002. Approaching English language research[M]. Singapore: Singapore University Press.

Berkenkotter C, Huckin T N. 1993. Rethinking genre from a sociocognitive Perspective[J]. Written Communication, 10(4): 475-509.

Berkenkotter C, Huckin T N. 1995. Genre knowledge in disciplinary communication: Cognitive, culture, power[M]. Hillsdale N J: L. Erlbaum Associates.

Bhatia V K. 1993. Analysing genre: Language use in professional settings[M]. London and New York: Longman Group.

Bhatia V K. 1997. The power and politics of genre[J]. World Englishes, 16 (3): 359-371.

Brett P. 1994. A genre analysis of the results section of sociology articles[J]. English for Specific Purposes, 13(1): 47-59.

Brown J D. 2001. Understanding research in second language learning[M]. Beijing: Foreign Language Teaching and Research Press.

Crookes G. 1985. Towards a validated analysis of scientific text structure[J]. Applied Linguistics, 7 (1): 57-70.

Dudley-Evans T, St John M. J. 1998. Development in ESP: A multi-disciplinary approach[M]. Cambridge: Cambridge University Press.

Dudley-Evans T. 1994. Genre analysis: an approach to text analysis for ESP[C]. In Coulthard. M (Ed.). Advances in Written Text Analysis. London and New York: Routledge.

Dusak A. 1990. Cross-cultural academic communication: a discourse-community view[J]. Journal of Pragmatics, 21: 291-313.

Evans K U H. 1998. Organizational patterns of American and German texts for business and economics: a contrastive study[J]. Journal of Pragmatics, 29: 681-703.

Feak C B, Reinhart S M, Sinsheimer A. 2000. A preliminary analysis of law review notes[J]. English for Specific Purposes, 19: 197-220.

Flowerdew J. 1993. An educational, or process, approach to the teaching of professional genres[J]. ELT Journal, 47 (4): 305-316.

Ghadessy M, Gao Yanjie. 2000. Thematic organization in parallel texts: the same and different methods of development[J]. Text, 20(4): 461-487.

Gibaldi J. 1999. MLA handbook for writers of research papers[M]. Shanghai: Shanghai Foreign Language Education Press.

Halliday M A K, Hansan T. 1985. Language, context, and text: aspects of language in a social-semiotic perspective[M]. Geolong, Vic.: Deakin University Press.

Henry A, Roseberry R L. 1996. A corpus-based investigation of the language and linguistic patterns of one genre and the implication for language teaching[J]. Research in the Teaching of English, 30 (4): 472-489.

Henry A, Roseberry R L. 1997. An investigation of functions, strategies and linguistic feature of the introductions and conclusions of essays[J]. System, 25(4): 479-495.

Henry A, Roseberry R L. 1998. An evaluation of a genre-based approach to the teaching of EAP/ESP writing[J]. TESOL Quarterly, 32 (1): 147-156.

Henry A, Roseberry R L. 2001. A narrow-angled corpus analysis of moves and strategies of the genre: 'Letter of Application'[J]. English for Specific Purposes, 20: 153-167.

Hoey M. 1983. On the surface of discourse[M]. George Allen & Unwin.

Holmes R. 1997. Genre analysis, and the social sciences: an investigation of the structure of research article discussion sections in three disciplines[J]. English for Specific Purposes, 16(4): 321-337.

Hopkins A, Dudley-Evans A. 1988. A genre-based investigation of the discussion sections in articles and dissertations[J]. English for specific purpose, 7(2): 113-122.

Hutchinson T, Waters A. 1987. English for Specific Purposes: a learning-centred approach[M]. Cambridge University Press.

Hyon S. 1996. Genre in three traditions: Implications for ESL. TESOL Quarterly, 30 (4): 693-722.

Kathepalia S. 1997. Cross-cultural variation in professional genres: a comparative study of book blurbs[J]. World Englishes, 16(3): 417-426.

McCarthy M. 1991. Discourse analysis for language teachers[M]. Cambridge University Press.

Noor Ronny. 2001. Contrastive rhetoric in expository prose: approaches and achievements[J]. Journal of Pragmatics, 33: 255-269.

Nwogu K N. 1991. Structure of science popularizaiton: a genre-analysis approach to the schema of popularized medical texts[J]. English for Specific Purposes, 10(2): 111-123.

Nwogu K N. 1997. The medical research paper: structure and function[J]. English for Specific Purposes, 16(2): 119-138.

Paltridge B. 1993. Writing up research: a system functional perspective[J]. System, 21 (2): 175-192.

Paltridge B. 1996. Genre, text type, and the language learning classroom[J]. ELT Journal, 50 (3): 237-243.

Paltridge B. 1999. The schematic structure of computer science research articles[J]. English for Specific Purposes, 18(2): 139-160.

Pery-Woodley, Marie-Paule. 1990. Contrasting discourses: contrastive analysis and a discourse approach to writing[J]. Language Teaching, 23 (3): 143-151.

Posteguillo S. 1999. The semantic structure of computer science research articles[J]. English for Specific Purposes, 18(2): 139-160.

Richards J, J Platt, H Weber. 1998. Longman Dictionary of Language Teaching & Applied Linguistics[M]. Beijing: Foreign Language Teaching and Research Press.

Salager-Meyer F. 1992. A text-type and move analysis study of verb tense and modality distribution in medical English abstracts[J]. English in Specific Purposes, 11: 93-113.

Samraj B. 2002. Introductions in research articles: variations across disciplines[J]. English for Specific Purposes, 21 (1): 1-17.

Scollon R. 2000. Generic variability in news stories in Chinese and English: a contrastive discourse study of five days' newspapers[J]. Journal of Pragmatics, 32: 761-791.

Seliger H W, Shohamy E. 1989. Second Language Research Methods[M]. Shanghai: Shanghai Foreign Languages Education Press.

Stein, Wayne. 1997. A Genre analysis of the TESOL conference abstracts[D]. PhD Thesis, Oklahoma State University.

Swales J, Najjar H. 1987. The writing of research article introductions[J]. Written Communication, 4 (2): 175-191.

Swales J M. 1990. Genre analysis: English in academic and research settings[M]. Cambridge: Cambridge University Press.

Swales J M, Feak B K. 1994. Academic writing for graduate students: Essential tasks and skills[M]. Ann Arbor: The University of Michigan Press.

Taylor G, Chen T. 1991. Linguistic, cultural, and subcultural issues in contrastive discourse analysis:

Anglo-American and Chinese scientific texts[J]. Applied Linguistics, 12(3): 319-36.

Valero-Garcés C. 1996. Contrastive ESP Rhetoric: Metatext in Spanish-English Economics Texts[J]. English for Specific Purposes, 15(1): 279-294.

Weissberg R, Buker S. 1990. Writing up research: Experimental research report writing for students of English[M]. London: Prentice-Hall International Limited.

Yang Ruiying. 2001. A genre analysis of research articles in applied linguistics[D]. PhD Thesis, National University of Singapore.

黄国文,葛达西,张美芳. 英语学术论文写作[M]. 重庆:重庆大学出版社,2009.

秦荻辉. 科技英语写作教程[M]. 西安:西安电子科技大学出版社,2009.

任胜利. 英语科技论文撰写与投稿[M]. 2版. 北京:科学出版社,2011.

王铭和. 英语科技论文写作[M]. 青岛:中国海洋大学出版社,2003.

辛书伟,王波. 英语科技文写作[M]. 天津:天津大学出版社,2003.

杨永林,杨芳,杨莉. 英语论文写作研究[M]. 北京:中央广播电视大学出版社,2002.

俞炳丰. 科技英语论文实用写作指南[M]. 西安:西安交通大学出版社,2003.

郑福裕,徐威. 英文科技论文写作与编辑指南[M]. 北京:清华大学出版社,2003.

朱月珍. 英语科技学术论文——撰写与投稿[M]. 2版. 武汉:华中科技大学出版社,2004.

本书例句范文选自如下期刊:

1. Applied Linguistics
2. Construction Innovation
3. Discourse Studies
4. ELT Journal
5. Engineering, Construction and Architectural Management
6. English for Specific Purpose
7. Environmental Conservation
8. Experimental Mechanics
9. Financial Services Review
10. Global Finance Journal
11. IEEE Transactions on Communications
12. IEEE Transactions on Computer-Aided Design of Integrated Circuits and Systems
13. IEEE Transactions on Computers
14. IEEE Transactions on Mobile Computing
15. IEEE Transactions on Systems, Man, and Cybernetics—Part C: Applications and Reviews
16. International Review of Economics & Finance
17. International Review of Financial Analysis
18. Journal of ACM
19. Journal of Applied Mechanics
20. Journal of Banking & Finance
21. Journal of Bridge Engineering
22. Journal of Composites for Construction
23. Journal of Computing in Civil Engineering
24. Journal of Construction Engineering and Management
25. Journal of Corporate Finance
26. Journal of Environmental Engineering

27. Journal of Financial Economics
28. Journal of Financial Markets
29. Journal of Heat Transfer
30. Journal of Irrigation and Drainage Engineering
31. Journal of Multinational Financial Management
32. Journal of Performance of Constructed Facilities
33. Journal of Pragmatics
34. Journal of Second Language Writing
35. Journal of Urban Planning and Development
36. Journal of Vibration and Acoustics
37. Journal of Water Resources Planning and Management
38. Practice Periodical on Structural Design and Construction
39. Quarterly Report of RTRI
40. Review of Financial Economics
41. System
42. TESOL Quarterly
43. The Journal of Strain Analysis for Engineering Design
44. The Shock and Vibration Digest
45. Transportation
46. Transportation Research—Part B: Methodological
47. Transportation Science
48. Vehicle System Dynamics
49. Water Environment Research
50. Written Communication